The Business of the Church

The Business of the Church

The Uncomfortable Truth that
Faithful Ministry Requires
Effective Management

John W. Wimberly, Jr.

THE
ALBAN
INSTITUTE
Herndon, Virginia
www.alban.org

The Alban Institute
2121 Cooperative Way, Suite 100
Herndon, VA 20171

Unless otherwise noted, all Scripture quotations are from the New Revised Standard Version of the Bible, © 1989, Division of Christian Education of the National Council of Churches of Christ in the United States of America, and are used by permission.

Cover design by Tobias Becker, Bird Box Design.

Library of Congress Cataloging-in-Publication Data

Wimberly, John W.

The business of the church : the uncomfortable truth that faithful ministry requires effective management / John W. Wimberly, Jr.

p. cm.

Includes bibliographical references.

ISBN 978-1-56699-404-0

1. Church management. I. Title.

BV652.W557 2010

254--dc22

2010009575

10   11   12   13   14   VP   5   4   3   2   1

Contents

Foreword   vii

Acknowledgments   ix

Introduction: The Ministry of Management   1

1. Managing Congregational Systems   7
2. Managing Personnel   39
3. Managing Facilities   71
4. Managing Church Finances   101

Conclusion: Congregational Management: A Holy Calling   143

Appendix A: A Sample Balance Sheet   147
Appendix B: A Sample Income Statement   151
Appendix C: Accounting Exercises   157

Notes   163

Foreword

John Wimberly has written an important book. He takes all of us who are involved in church life—as clergy, lay persons or staff—and shows us that managing a church is worth doing and worth doing well. He draws a straight and powerful line from effective church management to doing God's work.

Through the book we learn that managing the business aspects of the church is an important part of the whole and not the lesser part of a church's ministry. We can welcome the challenges involved and take meaning from the work we do rather than mourn the time we spend and the care we take.

Not only does John show us that managing a church well is important, he shows us how! How many times have we read management books where the author has some interesting conceptual ideas but doesn't (or can't) actually connect these ideas to practical application? With *The Business of the Church*, we see how a church is an interconnected system and how to be good stewards of each part of the system such that we have a healthy and well-functioning whole. John explains in clear and readable language the key aspects of managing a church and how they fit together, and he gives thorough yet succinct and practical instruction on how to approach each discipline.

And, *The Business of the Church* is a great read. John has a real gift for understanding people and relaying their stories, and these stories illustrate the book's concepts beautifully. They draw us in and leave us thinking about the book long after we've put it down. We see ourselves in these stories, and are inspired to think deeply about how we can apply what we learn from this book to our churches.

Stacy Brandom
Executive Vice President and Chief Financial Officer
Trinity Wall Street Episcopal Church
New York, New York

Acknowledgments

Thifs book is rooted in thirty-six years of ministry. I know what I know because of the many people with whom I've had the privilege to work over the years—staff colleagues, laypeople, judicatory folks, and many more. I cannot thank them enough for sharing freely with me and teaching me what they've learned about management in general—and church management in particular.

I am blessed to serve an amazing group of people at Western Presbyterian Church. They graciously choose to downplay my weaknesses and encourage my strengths. The same goes for my current group of gifted staff colleagues—Carol Howard Merritt, Gaston Paige, Shenella McGaskey, Tom Beveridge, and Ana Granados. They have all been very supportive of this book's creation.

My classmates and faculty in The George Washington University Executive MBA program taught me so much about how one can do business in an ethical and efficient manner. As I learned from them, I became committed to writing and teaching about the business life of the church.

Regarding the subject matter in the chapter on finance, I am in debt to Dr. Grant Clowery, an outstanding professor of accounting, who made sure my credits and debits were in order and made content suggestions as well. I also welcomed the insights of John Smithers, a dedicated local church treasurer. In the facilities chapter, I am grateful for Jim and Frankie Pangle, who shared their wisdom, accumulated over a lifelong career of caring for church facilities through their company.

I am very grateful to the Alban Institute for appreciating the importance of the subject matter in this book. Alban's deep experience in the life of congregations enabled them to see the importance immediately. Alban also gave me two outstanding editors, Andrea Lee and Doug Davidson, who provided invaluable ideas and suggestions in terms of organizing the material, content, and meticulous copyediting.

Finally, I thank my wife, Phyllis, for whom I have been missing-in-action for extended periods of time as I thought about and created this book. She is simply God's greatest gift to me in every way.

introduction

The Ministry of Management

As a pastor serving in congregational ministry for the past thirty-six years, I have been practicing business management daily. While most pastors don't tend to think of our work in these terms, management is an essential part of the job for every clergyperson. I'm writing this book for other pastors with whom I share this amazing vocation, in hopes we will be the best possible stewards and managers of the resources God has entrusted to us.

The seeds for this project were planted when I began an Executive MBA program in 2001. Having spent my entire professional life in the ministry, I thought I would be in over my head regarding managerial experience. My classmates were all thirtysomething, midlevel managers in major corporations. What did I know about management compared to them? However, I quickly learned that my own management skills and experiences rivaled most of theirs. My guess is that many other pastors could say the same.

As pastors, we manage buildings, finances, information technology, and personnel. We learn as we go. However, our task would be easier if we, as the church, discussed management more explicitly.

A number of great books have been written about leadership and strategic planning in the church. Yet very little has been written about effectively and faithfully managing the church. The *African American Church Management Handbook* has some excellent content and is widely used in the African American church.[1] But in my research, I found that most other books on the topic of church management either offer very little management "meat" or tend to view management as administration (a fundamental misunderstanding). So in this book, I stick to the subject of management—specifically, management of finances, personnel, and building and facilities. If good management takes place in the congregations we serve, we will be more faithful and productive stewards of the gifts God bestows upon our churches.

Over and again, Jesus called his followers to be faithful stewards. Good stewardship requires good management. Therefore, every pastor in congregational ministry needs to develop the essential skills to manage effectively.

Certainly, the life and teachings of Jesus demonstrate an explicit and unapologetic theology of management. His parables include stories of servants who invested aggressively rather than passively, stewards who watched faithfully over a large agricultural business, and a shepherd who made a risky decision to pursue a lost sheep (leaving ninety-nine to find one is not the safe management option!). When the disciples failed to supply enough food for a crowd, Jesus got a little irritated and took the management of the feeding into his own hands. Why did he waste his time on such mundane matters, on management? Because it wasn't a waste of his time! The physical aspects of ministry are as important as the "spiritual" aspects. Indeed, to embrace the physical and spiritual aspects of our work is to embrace the incarnational nature of our ministry.

The importance of church management is magnified when we understand that the Christian church is the original, largest, and wealthiest multinational corporation in the world. Almost two thousand years before Citibank, GE, or Microsoft, the church began to accumulate assets and personnel. By the sixteenth century, the Medicis of Florence had become Europe's richest family by managing the Vatican's money.

Today, the Christian church owns hundreds of millions of acres and hectares of property, including prime real estate sites in the centers of the world's richest cities. The church has a cash flow of billions of dollars annually. It has millions of employees. Indeed, it would take a great deal of research to find a country or region where the multinational corporation called the church doesn't have a local branch operation. Would any other large corporation dare to operate without making certain it had skilled managers in place? So why does the church send its managers (both clergy and lay) into the field without management training and support?

In my role as a manager, I find it helpful to keep in mind some overarching concepts. Those concepts will guide my approach in this book. They are:

- *The Church as a System.* A congregation is a system existing within the larger system(s) of our society. Within the congregational system are smaller systems, including facilities, financial, administrative, and personnel systems. All these smaller systems interact, shaping the life of the larger congregational system. If we manage systems, we will be far more effective.

- *The Church as a Business.* The state certainly understands the church as a business, requiring churches to incorporate as nonprofit organizations. Do those of us within the church have a similar understanding? *Business* is not a dirty word; it is a descriptive word. As businesses, our churches should have transparent financial operations, ethically sound personnel practices, and effective facilities management.

- *The Pastor as Manager.* Pastors are trained to be leaders. There are some interesting distinctions between leaders and managers that I will unpack in the book. As a starter, consider this definition of management by Peter Drucker: "Management is about human beings. Its task is to make people capable of joint performance, to make their strengths effective and their weaknesses irrelevant."[2] Drucker's definition of managing sounds a lot like Jesus's ministry!

Many examples in this book are drawn from my own experiences over nearly four decades of congregational ministry. These include real stories from churches I've served, as well as composites where I've changed names to protect the participants' identities. This book is also informed by countless conversations I've had with other pastors whose management skills have taught me much, as well as by my studies of management in and following my Executive MBA program.

I have been intentional in including examples from congregations of all sizes. Management is not confined to megachurches or even multiclergy staffed congregations. Every congregation has a program to manage, and most have a church that must be maintained. Many of us have secretaries, building maintenance people, and contractors to oversee. The issues involved in good financial management are exactly the same whether the church budget is $100,000 or $2,000,000. Managing information technology is a must for every congregation. So this book is for every pastor, not a select few.

While my primary intended audience is clergy, my hope is that this will also be helpful to laypeople entrusted with management tasks in the church. In a similar way, while I'm writing primarily for those serving Christian congregations, the content can easily be translated and applied by individuals serving religious congregations of other faiths.

My goal is to generate a broad discussion within the church regarding the importance of management. In seminaries, judicatories, and local congregations, we need to be discussing how we can most effectively manage the people, programs, and properties with which God has entrusted us. I am not so much invested in a particular set of management tactics as I am in elevating an awareness of our role as managers.

My hope is that the book will ignite a passion for developing management skills in congregations. Personally, I have found it fun to manage complex systems such as a building or church finances. Of course, it can get frustrating. When the contractor doesn't do the job correctly and I spend months ensuring that it gets done properly, it doesn't always feel like fun.

However, it is in moments of frustration that I remember what's at stake in congregational management. The better congregations manage their assets, the more assets they can give back to God and hand on to the next generation of church members. If giving back to God more than we were given doesn't sound important, I don't know what does.

chapter 1

Managing Congregational Systems

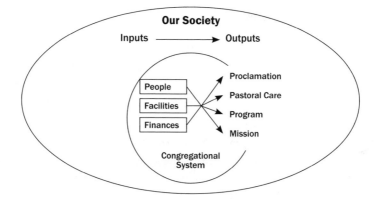

FIGURE 1.1. Inputs and Outputs in a Congregational System

A congregation is more effective and efficient in fulfilling the purposes God intends for it when the pastor manages the congregation as a system. Like the manager of a successful secular business, a managing pastor looks for the interdependence and interaction between a system's parts and the whole as well as the relationship required between three basic systemic inputs—people, facilities, and finances—to achieve desired outputs such as proclamation, pastoral care, program, and mission. If we fail to think about parts in relationship to their system and a system in relation to its parts, we miss very basic realities about the manner in which the system is functioning or malfunctioning. Paul made this point to the first century church when he used the image of a body and its parts to describe the church as the body of Christ. He said that without the important and seemingly not so important parts working together effectively, the larger body will suffer. Of course, the most important input is God's hand at work in and through the congregation!

The diagram on the next page reveals the systemic relationships that pastors as managers need to understand. The congregation exists within the larger system of society; the congregation has systems within it; and the congregational system requires specific inputs to get the desired ministry outputs.

In this chapter, we will examine three key points regarding a pastor's role in managing a congregation:

First, *a systems approach to management is useful to congregational management and ultimately, congregational health.* A systems approach can reveal the interrelationship of component parts with one another and the whole, making it easier to identify areas of congregational dysfunction and effective solutions. Such an emphasis encourages us to consider what inputs are needed (people, facilities, and finance) to generate the desired ministry results (such as proclamation, pastoral care, program, and mission). A systemic approach can also help us discover the ways in which anxiety exacerbates congregational dysfunction.

Second, *for pastors, other staff, and lay leaders to effectively manage a congregational system, a congregation needs a strategic plan.* A strategic plan helps a congregation measure its progress as well as identify and prioritize resources. It becomes the glue that keeps the parts working in harmony rather than against one another. Good managers use the plan as a reference point to see if the congregation's work has veered away from or is effectively working toward the plan's objectives. Managers direct staff and volunteers to the parts of the plan for which each party is responsible.

Third, *in a congregational system, the pastor's role and responsibilities as manager vary, depending upon the congregation's denominational polity, its membership size and constitution, and the size and configuration of its staff. By understanding the many, varying relationships and responsibilities of a manager, a pastor serving as head of staff fulfills them more effectively.* The pastor's relationships with the congregation, its governing board, and its committees vary greatly within the Christian community. Sizes of congregations and staffs vary greatly. When the lines of responsibility are clearly defined, the manager pastor resembles the conductor of a symphony, making sure all the inputs are present to create the desired output and then bringing out the best in the performers. Good managers love harmony!

Management and leadership are not one and the same even though they sometimes coexist in the same person. Understanding the difference between the two enables a pastor to differentiate between when she is managing or leading. Every head of staff needs to ask herself or himself: Does a particular situation call for leadership, management, or both? If both are needed, can I do both—or do I fulfill the role of either leader or manager and find someone else to do the other?

Systems Theory and Congregational Management

The leadership of St. John's Church couldn't believe the number and urgency of problems they were experiencing. They felt like Job. Suddenly and seemingly out of nowhere, they had major roofing problems; the director of Christian education had resigned; and a huge cash flow crisis occurred because several large bills had to be paid during the summer when member pledge payments were lower. Although the DCE's departure created some budgetary flexibility, it didn't make up totally for a cash crisis exacerbated by the unexpected roof problems.

A string of bad luck? Perhaps, but more likely these events reflected a systemic management failure at St. John's. A poorly maintained automobile or home usually has multiple problems. Poorly managed congregations also tend to have management-related problems pop up across the entire system. The various problems at St. John's had a common denominator. There was a failure to plan for and carefully manage the key inputs of ministry—adequate financial, people, and building resources. As a result, the output of their ministry was seriously crippled.

After dealing with their crises, the leadership at St. John's needed to evaluate how they were managing people, buildings, and money. Personnel don't just resign. Abrupt resignations are usually the result of frustrations that build up over time. Roofs don't just fail. They deteriorate over time. Cash flow emergencies don't just spring up out of nowhere. They are preventable with sound financial forecasting and the creation of adequate financial reserves.

These "unrelated" problems at St. John's were very much related. Good management pays attention to the inputs required for successful ministry, blending the various parts into a smoothly functioning congregational system. In the case of St. John's, it should have been maintaining or replacing the roofs in a timely manner (and making sure funds are set aside for emergency building repairs); communicating daily with personnel so frustrations were addressed on an ongoing basis; and creating an annual cash flow forecast that scheduled all major, expected cash outlays.

Ineffective managers run from one part of a system to the next, treating every problem and possibility as if it is unrelated to all the other parts of the system. Because the leadership at St. John's thought of its ministry as a bunch of unrelated, individual parts, it missed the complex, systemic interconnections between apparently diverse ministry inputs like roofs and staff members. If we think in terms of systems, we are much more likely to develop a comprehensive approach to management in our congregations. With an eye to the desired outputs of ministry, effective managers see the relationships between parts of a system and the entire system.

A METAPHOR FOR MANAGEMENT

Given Christian theology, the church should be a natural at thinking systemically. In seminary, pastors learned incredibly rich images describing who the church is and is called to be. In the New Testament, the church is described as the body of Christ (Eph. 1:22), the household of God (Eph. 2:19), and the church of the living God (1 Tim. 3:15), to name a few. These wonderful images help us understand the church in different ways.

When managing, I most enjoy envisioning the church as the body of Christ. A human body is a complex, interdependent system. As Paul so accurately described, when one part of the body fails or is undervalued, all the other parts struggle. So it is with the system we call the church. As we approach the subject of management, it is helpful to keep Paul's image in mind. When we attempt to manage staff, the buildings, finances, or anything else in our local congregations, we need to see all these inputs for ministry in the larger context of the system that is the body of Christ. If we don't, we will continually be treating symptoms and failing to treat the systemic problems that generate the symptoms.

In Romans 7:15, Paul wrote, "I do not understand my own actions. For I do not do what I want, but I do the very thing I hate." In like manner, leaders and managers of the church will never fully understand why the church does some of the holy and damnable things it does. However, with systems analysis, we gain key insights into the body of Christ's systemic behavior. As managers, this wisdom enables us be less judgmental and more understanding, less anxious and more assured, less arrogant and more humble.

THINKING SYSTEMICALLY

When it comes to systems theory, I, like so many others, have been heavily influenced by the work of Rabbi Edwin Friedman. Rabbi Friedman played a number of roles in my life, including friend, teacher, and therapist. In each role, Ed introduced me to different dimensions of systems theory.

Ed always framed individual issues in the larger framework of the systems in which we live, move, and have our being. He insisted the only way to approach any problem, change, or opportunity was to think within the larger context in which the problem or opportunity presented itself. As a result of Ed's influence, I have been a longtime, diehard convert to systems thinking.

Early in our friendship, I asked Ed for advice regarding two parents who came to me about their troubled adolescent. Their son was doing poorly in school and exhibiting antisocial behavior and other problems. Ed immediately said, "Tell the parents it isn't just their son who has a problem. These parents have a problem, too—and they need help just as badly as the son does. It is the family's systemic problem, not solely the individual's problem."

In like manner, congregations tend to isolate problems rather than viewing issues from a broader, systemic perspective. A forty-year-old boiler dies, and the congregation scrambles desperately for money to replace it. Didn't that congregation understand its dependence on that boiler for heat in the winter? Didn't they know the boiler would fail one day? If they did know, why didn't they plan for its replacement? This congregation's problem wasn't the boiler. It was a failure to think systemically about what they need to be successful in ministry.

In his classic book *Generation to Generation*, Friedman applied systems theory to the lives of religious congregations.[1] He makes an almost irrefutable argument that viewing a congregation as a system is the only truly effective way to understand and guide a congregation's behavior. In my opinion, this book is a must-read for any pastor and congregational leader.

MANAGING ANXIETY IN SYSTEMS

Friedman became convinced that systems, especially congregational systems, are dominated by anxiety-management issues. Good managers understand when and why anxiety rises or falls in the congregation and its members, as well as in the society in which the congregation ministers. They take into consideration the impact anxiety has on decision making and organizational behavior. Failure to address anxiety-based issues can cripple a congregation's ability to transform its ministry inputs into ministry output.

Anxiety is infectious. In systems, anxiety can travel top-down, bottom-up, or horizontally. Individuals operating within anxious societal systems or anxious congregational systems are more likely to be anxious themselves. If anxiety is not managed properly,

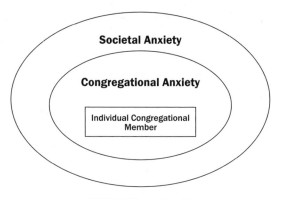

FIGURE 1.2 Systemic Anxiety

anxious church members can spread their anxiety to an entire congregation.

When discussing the impact of anxiety on a system, Ed loved to use the example of one of his relatives. Ed said that his anxiety level would immediately jump up several notches whenever he walked into this family member's house. Ed compared her and the millions like her to step-up transformers in electrical generation systems. A step-up transformer takes low voltage and raises it to a higher voltage. Ed's relative routinely took a low anxiety situation and magnified it into a high anxiety situation.

Continuing with the metaphor, Ed described other people who are step-down transformers. The voltage going through the wires on our streets is too high for household use. Therefore, each home requires a step-down transformer to lower the voltage. In every congregation are people who can reduce or step-down the system's anxiety.

"What are we going to do?" "What will happen if we fail?" "What if we choose the wrong option?" These questions and others like them are step-up transformers of anxiety when facing management decisions.

"Just as God cares for lilies of the field and birds of the air, so God will care for us." "This congregation has been through a civil war and world wars, economic depressions and recessions. We'll survive this problem." Such affirmations are step-down transformers of anxiety.

For Friedman, it's a given that anxiety exists in every system. Whether you are more of a step-up personality type or step-down type, you must realize that you can never eliminate all anxiety from a system. But the best managers learn to work with the anxiety—increasing, reducing, and shaping its impact to benefit the system as a whole.

In my opinion, it is a mistake to assume that step-up people are unhelpful while step-down people are helpful. A heightened anxiety level is a perfectly responsible and appropriate response to certain situations. If a lion is poking its head in the tent, it is appropriate to have someone say anxiously, "We're going to die unless we do something *now!*" If a congregation has a major financial problem, someone needs to raise the level of concern—and sometimes a manager may need to play this role if no one else is doing so. Yet good managers acknowledge, respond to, and deal with anxiety. By so doing, they reduce anxiety to appropriate levels and increase the productivity of the system.

In my experience, managers are especially likely to face anxiety-related problems when dealing with certain issues in congregational systems.

- *Church finances* can be difficult to understand until one has gone through several budgetary cycles. As a result, new people, in particular, often get very anxious when first serving on a finance committee. The only way I know to deal with this is to have a staff person or seasoned committee member spend a lot of one-on-one time with new members showing them the ins and outs of a congregation's financial realities. Orientation sessions are fine, but they have their limits. Finances are generally learned as one goes through a budgetary cycle. New members to a finance committee need to learn when regular payments are made for things like insurance, service contracts, and benevolences; the cash flow cycle of a congregation (usually this involves cash flow problems in the summer when people are on vacation); how special gifts and bequests are handled; and what restrictions, if any, are placed on various funds. It can be helpful for new members to review several years' worth of recent history of various key accounts such as building maintenance, utilities, and personnel. Constant mentoring helps manage anxiety rooted in financial issues.

- *"Deferred maintenance"* creates huge anxiety or massive denial (which is anxiety gone subterranean). I put "deferred maintenance" in quotes because it sounds so benign. In fact, "deferred maintenance" is no maintenance. Things that need to be maintained today aren't being maintained. Unless a congregation creates a plan to handle large maintenance issues that will rise up as surely as the sun does (boilers dying, roofs deteriorating, electrical panels needing to be updated, computers needing replacement), it will continually have to deal with the anxiety of members who realize that not having such a maintenance plan is like playing Russian roulette with the building and budget.
- *Personnel costs* create anxiety, especially during difficult financial times. This is especially true among staff members who begin to wonder if their jobs are secure. When a congregation enters a shaky financial time, members of the staff may begin to lobby laypeople to protect their jobs. This leads to very unhealthy factionalism within the congregational system. To manage this type of anxiety, the pastor and finance committee chair need to meet with staff regularly during rough economic times, explaining how the church plans to retain the current staff structure or, if cuts are imminent, what criteria will be used for reducing staff. This won't eliminate the anxiety. But it is a fair and just way to manage anxiety and support the staff.

In business school one of my professors said, "Businesses want to know what the near future will be. It can be bad. It can be good. But anything is better than the unknown. Thus, business fears chaos more than it fears bad forecasts." In other words, lack of knowledge about the near future creates anxiety.

When we deal with anxiety head on, we diffuse its divisive, fractious impact on the life of a congregational system. Not everyone will agree with every plan being proposed. But they will understand there is a plan. The anxiety level moves toward appropriate ranges as plans are implemented in reasonable and predictable ways.

THE CONGREGATIONAL SYSTEM
AND THE LARGER SOCIETAL SYSTEM

In addition to understanding the congregational systems they manage, pastors need to know the larger societal system of which all congregations are a part. In Romans 12:2 Paul advises, "Do not be conformed to this world, but be transformed by the renewing of your minds, so that you may discern what is the will of God—what is good and acceptable and perfect." Accepting that the church is a part of a larger societal system does not mean congregations need to accept all the values of the worldly system. We do not have to be "conformed to this world." But we are naive in the extreme if we do not acknowledge and understand the way the societal system affects our ministries.

How many managers predicted the Great Recession of 2008–2009? Surely, more of us should have seen it coming. But the magnitude of the financial system's collapse was both shocking and surprising to most. Many congregations suffered because they had not adequately prepared for a significant crisis in the larger societal system in which our smaller systems operate.

The church I serve here in Washington, D.C., is a case in point. For years, Western Presbyterian Church has been taking an aggressive amount of money out of its endowment to pay for exciting and important mission projects. Neither I nor the people I serve are big believers in growing an endowment for the sake of growing an endowment. Therefore, we have used the earnings from the endowment for mission rather than stockpiling them. With those earnings, we helped fund the first African American suburban new church development in our Presbytery's history, funded a local campus ministry, enabled a congregation in Ghana to grow from two hundred to two thousand in worship, and supported our feeding program for the homeless, to name a few of our major benevolence projects.

We did all this during a time when the larger, global economic system was experiencing enormous, rapid, and sustained growth. But all good things come to an end—and sometimes they come to a crashing, sudden end, as they did in the winter of 2008–2009. The collapse of the financial markets exposed our church's over-reliance on its endowment to fund major mission projects as well as the life of the congregation itself. Western had left itself too vulnerable to the harsh realities of a market crash. I'm grateful that the congregation's leadership was able to regroup without doing damage to the fundamentals of its ministry. But with more strategic consideration of the larger system in which it ministers, Western could have protected itself better.

The challenge of getting people to serve on church committees provides another example of how we are affected by the larger system in which we minister. In an urban community such as Washington, D.C., many church members don't get home from work and picking up their kids until 6:00 or 7:00 P.M. If committees meet in the evenings, these individuals can't come. If committees meet on weekends, they intrude on the only time some church members have with their families. How do we balance the needs of our congregational systems with the needs of our members' family systems?

Fundraising must also be viewed within the larger societal system. When I was growing up in the 1950s and 1960s, my parents gave to the church and maybe a little to several small charities. However, in today's society, we are inundated with requests to give to higher educational institutions and charities dedicated to everything from the environment to civil liberties. So congregational stewardship planning needs to be rooted in the realities of the larger system in which we operate.

THE LIMITS OF A SYSTEMS APPROACH

While a systems approach to management is crucial, I'm wary of any theory that claims to possess a comprehensive explanation of reality, of how we make decisions and act. Life is filled with too many exceptions (as well as the exceptional) to be explained by any one theory.

Good managers are skilled not only at figuring things out but also at knowing what they can't figure out. We don't need to and can't explain everything. When we look for and respect the mysterious, unexplainable factors present in all organizational and human behavior, we are likely to be less rigid in our managing. This flexibility helps us stay the course when events and people don't conform to our tidy, carefully designed systems charts. As I manage the system called Western Presbyterian Church, systems theory is the most frequently used item in my church management toolkit—but it's not the only tool.

Looking at congregational systems I have served and others with which I am familiar, I find myself considering questions that flow from systems theory: What in this congregational system causes a committee to fail time and time again? What dissuades this congregation from caring for its property in a manner comparable to the way the members care for their own homes? What in this system causes the members to ignore the church's need for the same kind of personnel policies they would demand in their own workplaces?

Over the years I have been amazed at the way systems thinking has allowed me to predict and, therefore, manage certain behavior in our family and congregation, as well as other systems. I don't believe in predestination. However, if systems are not understood and managed properly, they can produce results that feel and are, to a degree, predestined—not by God but by a system's all-too-predictable behavior.

Systems analysis helps us predict how systems will perform. If a dysfunctional system is unchanged, the outcomes it produces are predictably predetermined. For example, if we don't spend money to maintain a building today, we will spend even more money in the future to make needed repairs—or the building will become so dysfunctional it will be condemned. However, if we take charge of our systems by making faithful, effective leadership and management choices, outcomes can, to a fascinating degree, be guided. From his words to the adulteress woman to "go and sin no more" to his advising the rich ruler to give away his material possessions,

Jesus stressed that the choices we make determine the quality and character of our lives. Nowhere is this more evident in the choices we make as we lead and manage the church.

The Power of a Plan

Managing in a congregational system (or any other system) requires an overall framework for evaluating and making management decisions. By creating a strategic plan, a congregation provides its manager pastor with such a framework.

Peter Drucker was one of the primary developers and popularizers of management and leadership theory. Regarding strategic planning, he wrote: "Strategic planning is not forecasting. It is not masterminding the future. Any attempt to do so is foolish; the future is unpredictable."[2] As managers, strategic planning is essential precisely because we cannot forecast the future.

In strategic planning, congregational leaders shouldn't fool themselves into thinking they can forecast the future accurately. At best, we can make provisional bets about what the future will bring. Managers attempt to make good on those bets, while constantly evaluating and reevaluating their nature and accuracy.

Congregations need strategic plans because they guide the decisions managers will make. I like to say, "We manage to the plan." Every decision a pastor makes as a manager should relate to and help realize the congregation's strategic plan. *Every* decision.

A strategic plan lays out a vision for the future accompanied by broad objectives that, if accomplished, move the congregation closer to its vision. To the objectives are attached specific implementation strategies. Each of the strategies is assigned appropriate performance measurements (such as attendance in worship, new member growth, or number of pastoral visits) that will allow managers and leadership to evaluate whether or not strategies are being implemented successfully.

Too often, performance measurements are the missing element in church strategic plans. Why? My theory is that staff and committees are afraid they won't meet the performance goals and will be judged as failures. This fear reflects a shallow understanding of success and failure in an organization.

An inability to realize a particular performance goal may indeed mean the staff or committee didn't do its job effectively. However, it may also be possible, even likely, that the goal was unrealistic or the strategy was a poor one that should have been rethought or discarded. It wasn't the staff or committee that failed. It was a flawed strategy or a poor measure of performance.

Larger systems affecting our congregational lives need to shape strategic planning processes. While planning, we need to evaluate risks in the economic and societal systems within which we minister, gathering as much information as we can about the future, including information about the external systems that affect our ministry. At times these external systems will be sources of stability in our planning. At other times, they will be huge wild cards.

The Great Recession left a number of congregations around the nation in catastrophic situations. They'd made deals in which real estate developers were allowed to tear down their church buildings and redevelop the site for mixed commercial use as well as new office, worship, and program space for the congregation. When the real estate market collapsed, some developers went bankrupt— and their congregational partners were left holding the bag. One congregation now has a big excavation hole where their church building used to be located. A new building was supposed to be built there, with space for their congregation. But with a bankrupt developer mid-construction, who will complete the project?

Realities external to the congregation matter. Well thought-out strategic plans for these congregation-developer deals would have included not only the vision of a new church building built into a development project, but also objectives and strategies that took into consideration key external values like the possibility of a sudden tightening of the market or a real estate collapse. (Our current crisis isn't the first real estate collapse in U.S. history. They happen regularly.)

In strategic planning and its implementation, vision and objectives spring from and belong in the realm of leadership. Strategies and performance measurements are the stomping ground of managers. They are the GPS that guides managers in their decision making.

LEADER AND MANAGERS

With a strategic plan in place, a congregation's clergy and lay leaders nurture the vision and objectives, making sure they motivate and guide the church. They go to work implementing the strategic plan's specific strategies. The plan's performance measurements represent the envisioned outputs. The responsibility of the manager— whether lay or clergy—is to gather, utilize, and coordinate the inputs needed to realize the outputs.

Because the differences between leadership and management are often misunderstood, let us define and discuss them briefly:

- A *leader* is a visionary. She has a dream of what her congregation can be. He is a motivator. She can mobilize church members and staff around a vision.
- A *manager* is a person who can transform a vision into reality. She is a master at implementation. He gets the job done, by dealing with all the nitty-gritty, day-to-day issues that make or break a congregation. She attends to and follows through on the details many leaders find boring or distracting or don't even notice.

Although these definitions present a sharp contrast between leaders and managers, in real life, most leaders possess some managerial skills and most managers have some leadership abilities. The smaller the congregation, the more essential it may be for the pastor to fulfill both roles. Yet this artificially sharp contrast between leaders and managers can help pastors clarify the differences between the leadership and management responsibilities in a congregation and evaluate whether their own gifts are weighted more in the direction of leadership or management.

While some individuals in the church have both of these skills in abundance, most of us tend to have more of one than the other.

For example, Martin Luther King Jr. was primarily a leader. He had an inspiring, prophetic vision that he broke down into clear objectives such as civil rights legislation and fair housing and employment practices. As a great leader, he knew how to galvanize people into action around a vision. But he also had the wisdom to know he was not a manager. Building the civil rights movement state by state and county by county was not his forte—and he knew it. So King surrounded himself with individuals who had excellent management skills. The civil rights movement succeeded due to a remarkable collection of gifted leaders (whose names we tend to remember) and highly skilled managers (whose names most of us don't know).

While serving a congregation in Houston in the mid-1970s, I heard about a nearby church that was experiencing remarkable growth. As a young pastor wanting to know the keys to congregational success, I sought out and met the pastor. I was surprised at his lack of charisma. He didn't impress me as a leader-type. "Why do so many people find him so compelling?" I wondered.

As I learned about his ministry, I realized people were drawn to this church not because of the charisma of its pastor leader but because of its very effective, focused congregational ministry. The pastor was the consummate manager, doing all the organizational things needed for the congregation to grow. He was a master at taking care of the system.

Harvard University Business School professor John Kotter suggests that leadership and management "both involve deciding what needs to be done, creating networks of people and relationships that can accomplish an agenda, and then trying to ensure that those people actually get the job done."[3] A church leader wonders, "What does God want us to do in this situation? How is our environment for ministry changing? How can we be more responsive to the needs of our members and the world?" In answering the questions, the leader will consider broad cultural patterns, theological crosscurrents, and sociological trends, as well as the congregation itself. In short, the leader is a strategic thinker. Managers gravitate toward what exists and draw conclusions from their observations. They ask, "Where do we get the money to fund this project? How long will it take? Can we find the human

	LEADER	MANAGER
Thinking	Inductive	Deductive
Mindset	Likes creative chaos, wants movement in the organization, works long term	Likes creating order, wants consistency, works short term
Style	Establishing direction, motivating personnel, creating a strategic plan	Planning & budgeting, organizing & staffing, controlling & problem solving, implementing organization to the strategic plan and aligning staff to it

FIGURE 1.3 Differences Between Leaders and Managers

resources needed to succeed or are we overextending ourselves?" In answering the questions, managers compile data about things upon which they can rely. They highlight the givens and variables in any situation. As the variables grow more volatile, the manager grows more cautious.

In *A Force for Change: How Leadership Differs from Management*, Kotter provides numerous helpful insights for differentiating leadership from management. Other management scholars have joined Kotter in identifying some of the following distinguishing characteristics of managers and leaders.

The conflicting goals and styles of leadership and management can and will create conflict. Kotter notes, "Strong leadership, for example, can disrupt an orderly planning system and undermine the management hierarchy, while strong management can discourage the risk taking and enthusiasm needed for leadership."[4] Emotionally and spiritually healthy leaders and managers will turn this inherent conflict into a productive tension that benefits the congregation.

My experience is that most pastors are more comfortable in leadership roles rather than management. We like to move from one thing to the next, think about the big picture, and motivate people to accomplish significant goals. We are less thrilled with the management role; it feels tedious and repetitive. As a result, we are like a "good hit, bad fielding" baseball player. The preference of many clergy to lead rather than manage explains why many congregations are not managed optimally. As they put together their staffs and lay leadership teams, congregations can augment a pastor's preference toward being a leader or a manager. Strong clergy and lay leadership teams include a well-crafted blend of leadership and management abilities.

Pastors should constantly ask themselves, "Does this situation demand a leader or a manager?" If we approach a management problem from a leadership perspective, we are likely to mismanage it. If we approach a leadership problem from a management perspective, we are likely to miss opportunities to create positive change in the congregation. With an understanding of the differences between management and leadership, let us return to the subject of management in a system.

MANAGING INPUTS

"What do we want to do?" is a basic organizational question. It's a question focused on results, or output. Ford Motor Company, for example, envisions the output of sold cars. To get the desired output, it needs certain inputs, such as a means of production, capital, and a product distribution system. Viewed in terms of inputs and outputs, leaders envision outputs, but managers work with inputs to produce outputs.

St. Thomas Lutheran Church had identified certain desired outputs (objectives) in its strategic plan, including a strong Christian education program, an inspiring worship experience, and a diverse range of mission programs. The managers in the congregation identified three key inputs they needed to realize their plan: personnel, money, and buildings. The questions they asked are fundamental:

- Regarding personnel: How do we staff to fulfill these objectives? Do we use volunteers? Hire new staff? Revise the job descriptions of existing staff?

- Regarding money: How much money is needed to make this strategy work? Does it already exist in the budget? Or will a special fundraising effort be required?
- Regarding buildings: Is the congregation's building ready for this strategy? Does the church building need to be re-designed or space added? What kind of technology additions or upgrades will be required for the plan to succeed?

St. Thomas's success will depend not just on its vision but also on its management of the inputs. If the church manages the inputs effectively, it increases the chances of realizing its desired vision.

Good strategic planners advise congregations to do "less" better rather than "more" poorly. Such advice recognizes the reality of limited inputs. Some congregations have more inputs than others. But no matter the size of the congregation, inputs are always limited—*always*.

As they analyze a strategic plan, good managers need to be honest with the congregations they serve about the availability or lack of essential inputs. If a congregation can't mobilize the necessary inputs to achieve a desired output, then it should drop the accompanying strategy. A better strategy for mobilizing the inputs can always be developed.

Nowhere is the importance of the relationship between proper inputs and desired output more evident than in the military. In the mid 1990s, the U.S. Army released an analysis showing a need for 2.5 soldiers working on logistics to support every single combat soldier. Seventy percent of the personnel support the other 30 percent. The 30 percent are fulfilling the vision we usually associate with the military. But without the input of the 70 percent involved in logistics, the mission fails.

In like manner, a congregation can't expect to do its job without plenty of supporting inputs. Logistically, congregations need proper technology, building space, staff, and money. A congregation can plan all day and night. However, unless managers ensure that the needed inputs are present, nothing is going to happen.

While most inputs are tangible, communication is an intangible yet crucial factor within well-managed systems. People who don't know what they are supposed to do won't do it. People who aren't listened to can't communicate problems that prevent them from getting the job done. Since people are one of any organization's three crucial inputs, a lack of effective communication among people can be crippling to a congregation.

In 1982, business gurus Thomas Peters and Robert Waterman coined a term "management by walking around" that instantly became famous.[5] Peters and Waterman were critical of managers who sit in their offices and expect things to happen. They contend that managers need to be in constant contact with those they manage. Then and only then will they understand what their employees need (key inputs such as materials, training, money, and technology).

Pastor Jones was upset because he kept getting constant complaints about the church bathrooms not having sufficient toilet paper, soap, and paper towels. After another interruption as he tried to finish his sermon, he wondered, "Why do I have to deal with this kind of stuff?" The answer is because he didn't have a good management system in place. When Pastor Jones called the janitor into his office and asked him about the problem, he was told the secretary didn't order the supplies in a timely manner. When he called the secretary and asked her about it, she said the janitor didn't tell her he needed supplies until he'd run out of them. So the bathroom would lack essentials until she made a new order and supplies arrived.

If Pastor Jones had been managing by walking around, he would have heard about the problem from both employees and the "customers" (church members) long before it became a major issue. All he had to do was ask the employees what they needed to do their jobs better and easier. To a listening, responsive manager, the employees would have explained their problems and probably described several viable solutions.

Whether communication is created by staff meetings, management by walking around, conference calls, e-mail, walkie-talkies, pagers, Blackberries, or some other way, every congregational system needs an intentional, well thought-out strategy for creating and maintaining communication with and among employees.

Certainly, staff meetings can be very helpful in coordinating personnel. However, they have their limits when it comes to management. People with good verbal skills and those comfortable with conflict typically dominate staff meetings. This leaves out staff members who are conflict-averse or less verbal. To hear staff and congregational members who may not speak up in meetings, manager pastors need to be out of their offices and in the lives of the people they manage. One on one with employees and church members, they will hear things never spoken in a staff, committee, or congregational meeting.

Employees should not have to deal with problems by themselves. A good manager is seen as an ally by those she manages, and is available to help them think through challenging situations. If a congregation has staff who feel isolated and stranded, it has managers who have failed to devise a communication strategy allowing managers and managed to be plugged in to one another.

COMMON TRAPS

Peter Senge teaches organizational studies at MIT's Sloan School of Management. I find him to be a very practical scholar of organizational systems. Using a number of systems "archetypes," Senge has identified several common traps into which systems can fall.[6] Skilled managers know and are watching out for these traps. Seeing them on the horizon, they make plans to avoid falling into them. Senge views the most common systemic traps as limits to growth, shifting the burden, escalation, success to the successful, and growth and underinvestment.

Limits to Growth
Some congregational systems are very effective at managing the inputs that promote fairly rapid growth, such as good worship experiences, effective programming, and vital mission outreach. However, most systems also have built-in limits to membership growth that, when reached, will kick in and stop growth in its tracks—things like lack of seating in worship, lack of staff to

expand programming, or inadequate parking. Leaders often plan for continuing growth that won't happen because of the built-in limiting factors. We must recognize these limits, so we can either (1) live within the limits or (2) devise ways to transcend them. For example, Western has a rapidly growing children's Sunday school program. Every year, it requires more space. But space is limited. If Western doesn't think its way through this growth limit, it will hit a wall and stop growing. If the congregation's managers think creatively about the space they have, they should be able to find ways to sustain growth. However, they can't wait until the day the Christian education department hits the wall regarding current space configurations. Managing this issue is key to the congregation's future.

Shifting the Burden

Many systems tend to identify a problem and then employ an effective but short-term solution to the problem. Instead of employing a short-term solution that ultimately will fail, managers need to apply, from the beginning, long-term, systemic solutions to fundamental problems. For example, a congregation has a ten-year-old flat roof. There are continual problems because water stands on the roof, ultimately leading to leaks. (Think twice before accepting a call to any congregation whose building has a flat roof.) When a leak appeared in the sanctuary, the roofer offered two solutions. One option was to put a rubberized coating on the roof and then cover it with loose, gravel-like material. The manufacturer of this roofing product offers a free ten-year guarantee that can be extended for an additional five or ten years for a fee. The other option was to patch the current leak and continue to do the same as leaks reappeared. The cost of the rubberized roofing solution was $20,000. The cost of repairing the current leak was $1,500 for the roofer, plus whatever drywall and painting expense was needed to repair the interior damage. Most people would agree the long-term solution is best. But not every congregation can raise the $20,000. If this congregation doesn't have the money, one option would be to take out a loan. Even with interest, this approach might well be cheaper than continual spot repairs.

Escalation

Parts within a system can compete with one another. We sense this at play in Paul's descriptions of first-century congregations at war with themselves. When the parts compete, the battle escalates in ways that are destructive for the system as a whole. A recent example involved two daycare centers that rented space from First Baptist Church. It was a good deal for the daycare centers and produced crucial revenue for the congregation—until one of the centers asked the pastor about renting part of the space currently being used by the other. As word of this spread, a healthy, balanced system became unbalanced. The two centers began to compete for space. Afraid they might lose out, they also began looking for alternate space with other congregations. Unsure of their future in the church space, both daycare centers decided to relocate. The church was left with a gaping hole in its budget.

Managers ensure that parts complement rather than compete with one another. They make sure every part (and every person) in the system feels valued. By doing so, they keep things from needlessly escalating into lethal competition.

Success to the Successful

Systems have an almost automatic tendency to allocate more resources to those parts of the system that are "successful." This means fewer resources flow to other parts that are less successful yet equally crucial to the system's health. I would change Senge's terminology from *successful* and *less successful* to *obvious* and *not so obvious*. Sometimes we allocate resources to obvious opportunities and problems while ignoring not-so-obvious opportunities and problems. For example, when the stock market was thriving, the congregation I serve was not paying attention to some not-so-obvious potential savings in our budget. When the stock market crashed, Western had to scrutinize more carefully all our expenses. In the process, we discovered we could have been saving as much as $10,000 in annual insurance costs if we'd changed a few options in our policy. Those savings had been lying around for years, waiting for someone to take advantage of them. But because we were focused on the obvious (earnings from the endowment), we didn't do as good a job managing our expenses.

Growth and Underinvestment

This trap is an offshoot of the limits to growth scenario. It speaks specifically to a congregation's failing to invest in the things necessary to sustain growth in membership. Arlin Rothauge, Roy Oswald, Alice Mann, and others have identified the characteristics of various types of congregations by size (family, pastoral, program, and corporate).[7] Their work reveals how a congregational system changes as it grows, and that there are some systemic resistance points to growth that must be overcome at each stage for growth to continue. The underinvestment trap offers an additional reason why some congregations are unable to grow their membership: They fail to budget for the added staff and facilities that will be needed just beyond the horizon.

Church of the Covenant was growing rapidly—and unwittingly approaching a growth limit. The single pastor was on the verge of burnout and the congregation's governing board did not feel the church could afford to hire a second. If management recognized the situation as a growth limit and stretched finances to hire an additional pastor, it would have moved through the growth limit. But if it hesitated and waited until the limit was reached, the growth would stall and the application of additional resources would be too late. The pastor would burn out. The congregation's membership would begin to decline as the lack of adequate pastoral services became evident. Unfortunately, the congregation decided to be penny wise and pound foolish. Unwilling to spend the money needed to hire additional pastoral help, the congregation saw the pastor who was key to its growth choose to move to a larger church where he had more pastoral help.

Clearly, adding personnel is a very expensive option, and many congregations retreat from it. But this is a mistake for congregations seeking to grow. In the twenty-first century, the amount of time members can contribute to the church has real restraints. Churches may need to hire staff (part or full time) to continue a growth trajectory. Additional staff leads temporarily to a tight budgetary situation until the growth orchestrated by the new staff arrives. In the meantime, a manager needs to carefully analyze what expenses can be cut or delayed. Until the new revenues appear from new members, smart management of expenses can keep the books balanced.

This is a place where the church can learn from the business world. Companies that grow reinvest significant amounts of their profits back into the company so they can continue growing. In contrast, too often, the church hoards its growing finances rather than committing them to additional, future growth. Think of the hundreds of congregations that have allowed their endowments to grow while their mission and membership eroded.

The Importance of the Pastor as System Manager

Ken Lay and Bernard Ebbers, former CEOs of Enron and Worldcom respectively, tried to tell the world and the courts they didn't know what was going on in their companies. Contending they were leaders of their organizations, rather than daily managers, they claimed innocence regarding the rampant fraud in their corporations. Nobody bought their arguments. Ebbers was given a twenty-five-year prison sentence; Lay, who died before being sentenced, was convicted on ten counts of violating laws.

When things go terribly wrong in the life of a congregation, pastors who say they are leaders and not managers won't go to jail. However, their ministries probably won't survive the crisis. Their pleas that they weren't involved in the management decisions will rightly fall upon deaf ears. Many will end up leaving their congregations saying they were victims of "misunderstandings" or complaining that they took the fall for someone else's failure. It doesn't have to end this way.

The closest thing a congregation has to a CEO is its head of staff—the pastor. I do not confine the term *head of staff* to churches with multiple clergy. Solo pastors are also heads of staff. In small congregations, the staff may be all volunteer. However, the volunteer gardeners, Sunday school teachers, and building people definitely form a staff, and they all need a person to whom they report. Indeed, managing volunteers can be a greater challenge than managing paid staff.

A head of staff position is shaped by a number of different factors. Certainly, every denomination and each independent congregation has different expectations and regulations regarding the role of head of staff. In addition, the size of both the congregation and its staff changes the management issues confronting a head of staff. Many of the people the head of staff manages are volunteers. They may not be on payroll, but they are key to successfully implementing a strategic plan.

DENOMINATIONAL FACTORS

To seize the opportunity of being a head of staff, pastors need to assume managerial responsibility to the extent it is appropriate. "Appropriate" is determined by the possibilities and constraints of managerial expectations for pastors, which will vary widely from denomination to denomination, and from local congregation to local congregation.

It is beyond the scope of this book to examine the specific managerial responsibilities of a pastor in each Christian denomination. But one thing is true in every denomination: When a problem occurs in a congregational system where managerial responsibility is not well defined, the buck stops on the head of staff's desk. For this reason it is important to define who has final authority on managerial issues *before* a crisis presents itself. Furthermore, everyone needs to know and agree upon who has responsibility for each of the primary inputs into ministry.

Within a congregational system, does an individual or group have the management responsibility? Is it a staff person or a committee? Does the congregation's governing board function as a leadership group, a management group, or a bit of both? If both, what areas is the board supposed to lead? What areas should it manage?

Concerning the three inputs for ministry, who has the final managerial responsibility for personnel, finances, and building issues? In many polities, the managerial responsibility and authority for these may be divided among boards, committees, the pastor, and even individual church members. There is nothing wrong with these responsibilities being divided, as long as the divisions are made clear so everyone knows who is managing what.

In many congregations managerial responsibility and authority assigned constitutionally to a particular group can be delegated elsewhere. For example, in the Presbyterian system, the trustees are responsible for management of the building. However, preferring oversight to a managerial role, trustees often delegate their managerial responsibility to the pastor, business manager, or church janitor.

CONGREGATIONAL AND STAFF SIZE FACTORS

Allocation of managerial responsibilities will also be shaped by the size of the congregation and its staff. In the next chapter on personnel, I will discuss some of the ramifications of congregational and staff size for managing personnel. But there are also managerial authority issues relevant to a congregational system.

For example, in a small congregation, by default, the pastor is usually the primary manager. However, if a small congregation has a secretary, a staff person who cleans and maintains the building, or both, those individuals usually do some management in their discrete areas. In small congregations, laypeople play important management roles. Defining management responsibilities among the pastor, other staff, and key laypeople needs to be done carefully and clearly.

In a midsize congregation with two clergy on staff, the management responsibilities, if undefined, can get fuzzy. Failure to make clear definitions and divisions of labor leads to problems, including a lack of management or overmanagement in certain subsystems.

In one congregation I served as an associate pastor, the pastor's secretary had been handling the management of building staff. When I arrived, the head of staff wanted me to assume management of the building and its staff. Predictably, it didn't take long for the secretary and me to develop an adversarial relationship (despite liking each other personally). We finally sat down and sorted out who was in charge of what. With management responsibilities clarified, we lived happily ever after (more or less).

In a large congregation, management assignments are even more complicated. For example, while an executive pastor or business manager might oversee the staff, the senior pastor remains the head of staff. Again, that will become clear when a crisis occurs. Additionally, in large congregations, the layers of management necessarily increase. Associate pastors may become midlevel managers who oversee other part- or full-time workers such as youth or music ministers. As the layers of responsibility increase, so do the opportunities for misunderstanding and miscommunication. Knowing who is responsible for what becomes a major task in such a complicated staff system.

Communication is especially important among larger staffs. Staff meetings are an important time to ensure communication throughout the system. They can also be a time to coordinate the management of various subsystems of the larger congregational system. If such communication and coordination doesn't happen, parts of the system will quickly start working against one another or will overlap in ways that create significant inefficiencies and irritation.

In congregations of every size, clarity about the managerial role of the church board and congregational members is extremely important. In every church I have served, I have had some conflicts with members as I explained to them that I am the manager of the church's secretaries and building personnel. It is unfair to expect staff to respond to the management requests of hundreds of members; in effect, these staff members end up with hundreds of bosses. Church members who want a staff person to do something need to go to the head of staff or his or her clearly defined agent, who can pass along the request (if it is reasonable and needs to be done).

Managers need to make sure any wannabe managers in congregations understand (1) who has responsibility to assign work and (2) how to process work requests. When such management lines are clear, I have found that 95 percent of church members are glad to work within those defined rules. As for the other 5 percent . . . well, there is always that other 5 percent.

MANAGING VOLUNTEERS

Management of volunteers is at the heart of ministry. We can't fire them—and we can't get the work of the church done without them. So managing volunteers is a fundamental skill every pastor needs. The basic principles that guide management of volunteers are no different than those related to managing paid staff:

- Create clear job descriptions. What are they expected to do?
- Each volunteer needs to know where he or she goes with questions or problems.
- Volunteers need to be trained and oriented to their work.
- Are volunteers being recruited to serve "life sentences" or for a well-defined period of time?
- To avoid having every volunteer in the pastor's office asking questions or offering suggestions, volunteers generally should be organized into teams with one of their own assuming management of the team.

GETTING THE MOST FROM YOUR TEAM

To conclude this chapter on managing a system, let me return to the image of the conductor of a symphony. Conductors know what instruments and musicians are needed to play a particular piece of music. (They know the required inputs.) They know the strengths of the particular orchestra they are conducting. They coordinate the inputs to produce the best possible performance (output).

In like manner, managers in congregations assemble the inputs needed to produce the best performance of the system they are managing. They know that the necessary inputs of money, facilities, and people are essential, yet they are only the beginning of organizational success. Identifying the strengths and weaknesses of the individuals as well as of the system itself, a manager coordinates them in ways that maximize the ministry outputs of proclamation, pastoral care, program, and mission.

Just as the conductor doesn't play the oboe or violin herself, but enables all the musicians to play their instruments in harmony, so should it be with the congregational manager. We have all seen pastors who micromanage, trying to do themselves what the people they are managing should do. Such pastors are impossible, driving themselves and everyone around them crazy. They lose staff. They usually lose their jobs and rightfully so.

Sadly, few people think of Jesus as a manager. However, Jesus took a rag-tag group of people who chose to follow him and transformed them into a smoothly functioning organization. He didn't go find his own donkey for the trip into Jerusalem. He managed others who got the task done. Jesus didn't micromanage, going out with the disciples to every little town. He trained them, equipped them with what they needed to get the job done (precious little in the way of resources compared to ministry today), and then let them do the work given to them. This was more than divinely inspired leadership. It was divinely inspired management. Because he was fully human, he seems to have had fully the qualities of leadership and management.

Granted, the small organization Jesus founded nearly collapsed in the hours immediately following his arrest and crucifixion. With their leader gone and their hopes dashed, the disciples scattered "like sheep without a shepherd." But it is a testimony to Jesus's leadership and managerial skills that he was able to overcome his disciples' failure and pull his followers back together in the days following his resurrection. The reassembled disciples learned from their experience and made history-changing adjustments to their behavior.

In the years following Jesus's resurrection, they did more than preach and teach. They were planning and budgeting, organizing and staffing, controlling and problem solving, all in ways that resembled the managerial genius we see at work in Jesus's ministry. In no small part, all of this is the result of Jesus attending to the personnel needs of the church he created. He managed people in ways that can teach us much. In the next chapter, we will think about keys to successful management of people in today's church.

Manager's Checklist

- What biblical image would you use to describe your congregation as a system?
- Create a chart that graphically displays your congregation's system. This would include the many systems operating within the congregation such as the choir and prayer groups, the inputs into the system(s), and the outputs from the system (desired and actual).
- Does your congregation have a strategic plan? If no, what in the system has discouraged one being created? If yes, do you manage to the plan? If no, why?
- What raises the anxiety level of your congregational system? How might increased anxiety be managed effectively?
- Is your congregation falling into any of Peter Senge's traps: limits to growth, shifting the burden, escalation, success to the successful, and growth and underinvestment? Which ones are most evident?

chapter 2

Managing Personnel

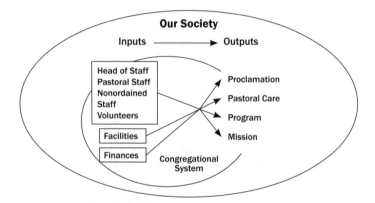

FIGURE 2.1 Personnel Inputs

The church is, first and foremost, about people. Therefore, we might expect churches to appreciate the importance of the management of people. However, the treatment of persons in our employ is too often less than salutary and, at times, downright unjust.

I don't want to set the corporate world on a personnel pedestal. However, the business community has given a lot of careful thought to and produced a great deal of literature on the subject of managing personnel. Although this has produced many different strategies and techniques, most people agree that good personnel management involves three things:

1. bringing people together to work effectively and efficiently for a common purpose,
2. helping people maximize their strengths and minimize the impact of their weaknesses,
3. training and developing the skills employees need to succeed in their work.

The quality of personnel practices within the business community varies. Nonetheless, most companies are aware of the employment laws they need to obey, the importance of handling hiring and firing decisions both ethically and legally, and the need for ongoing employee training. Many companies have commendable family leave policies. The best companies have complete personnel policies that are handed to new employees the day they are hired.

The failure of the church to employ some of the best practices used in the business community's personnel management has cost us dearly. On October 18, 2009, the Roman Catholic Diocese of Wilmington (Delaware) filed for bankruptcy. It was the *seventh* diocese to do so in recent years. Each of these bankruptcies was the result of sexual misconduct by priests. How could this happen? Flawed personnel management is at the heart of this disaster for the Catholic Church. The mismanagement was systemic rather than isolated; it took place from the top down as well as horizontally across the leadership of the church.

In the Presbytery where I have served for more than three decades, the severance packages paid to some clergy have crippled the ability of several congregations to minister effectively. Most of these pastors left because the call was a bad fit or because the congregation felt the pastor simply didn't get the job done. When those congregations were forced to pay more than a year's salary to the departing clergy, many of them had to cut their mission and program budgets or delay the hiring of a new pastor. Some of the mismatches between clergy and congregation could not be predicted or avoided. But too often, the poor fit reflected a failure of the calling congregation and the judicatory to thoroughly vet candidates. The business of the church was hurt by personnel mismanagement.

Well-managed systems don't allow an employee's misconduct to jeopardize the welfare and fiscal solvency of the entire organization. Rather than shuffling offenders from one department to another (as the church too often does by moving clergy from one parish to another), well-run organizations fire offending employees. By so doing, they send a clear message to other employees that violations of well-defined personnel policies will not be tolerated.

Since personnel is the largest single area of expense in most church budgets, we literally cannot afford to manage our personnel without using the best employment practices. Given that personnel problems almost always result in the loss of church members who feel the departing staff person was treated unjustly, we must work extra hard to make sure personnel are well managed. Given that the church is a "people organization," proper treatment of the people employed by the church needs to be at the top of our priorities. Every single congregation should have personnel policies and practices that reflect the values we teach and preach.

When clergy get together, they often complain about troublesome areas in the churches they serve. Some aspect of personnel management is usually among those complaints. There are complaints about the secretary who thinks that she, not the pastor, manages the church (even worse, maybe she does!); the choir director whose musical taste is driving visitors away (if choir members adore the director, a classic battle may ensue); the janitor who has a unique definition of the skill called "cleaning"; the associate pastor who believes he's called to give the congregation thirty hours a week, even though he's paid for forty or fifty hours. Clergy complain to their colleagues about ineffective, disruptive, and undermining staff members because they don't know what else can be done about them!

Building on the preceding chapter, we'll use a systems approach to understand the management of personnel—the first of the three key inputs into a congregational system. We'll focus on several key points:

- Churches need to be clear about who is managing whom.
- When personnel are evaluated in the context of the overall system with all of its interdependent and interacting parts, heads of staff better understand the way particular staff members function.
- Personnel and job descriptions need to be aligned to a congregational system's goals and managed to that end.
- The use of teams to manage involves not only changing the name of groups doing work in the church but also changing the manner in which people work together and managers manage.
- Good personnel policies are essential guides for managers and employees alike.

Don't expect any discussion of personnel, including this one, to provide foolproof solutions to the thorny personnel issues faced by most pastors and congregations. We are talking about hiring, compensating, motivating, supervising, and evaluating human beings. Since every human being is unique, the opportunities and challenges of managing each employee will be equally unique. That being said, human behavior can usually be grouped. Therefore, it is possible to develop standardized personnel policies that can be valuable for every manager and employee.

Who Is Managing Whom?

It's clear that all paid personnel in a congregation need to be managed. This includes associate and assistant pastors, pastoral interns, executive pastors, business managers, secretaries, building personnel, music personnel, and programmatic personnel.

The question for every church is: Who handles the supervision or management of each staff member? Staff members doing the managing will almost always include the solo or senior pastor of a multiclergy staff (whom we will refer to as head of staff). Typically, the pastor serving as head of staff would be responsible for managing any other pastors on the staff, even if all clergy are hired and dismissed by the congregation itself. In some cases management responsibilities may be part of the job descriptions of other staff, or these staff may be charged with these supervisory responsibilities by the head of staff. An executive pastor or business manager could be charged with managing the secretarial and building staff. In a very large church, programmatic staff may have management responsibilities. For example, the head of youth ministry may manage part-time workers in youth ministry, or the music director may manage the director of the children's choir.

It is essential that all employees be clear about who is managing whom. If the children's choir director is supervised by the music director, yet he feels he can go directly to the head of staff for guidance, it is no longer clear that the music director is the manager of the choir director. If an associate pastor isn't receiving proper guidance and feedback from the head of staff about the work she needs to do, she will be a confused rather than purposeful employee.

Church governing boards, personnel committees, and program committees can add to the management confusion. How much management responsibility do they have? In a medium to large church, the management responsibility of boards and committees should be quite limited. Most management should be done by staff. In a small church, laypersons are usually more involved in management—making it even more important that management lines of responsibility are clearly defined.

How limited is the management role of these groups of lay people? A personnel committee is of great service to a congregation when it creates clear personnel policies, advocates for fair, appropriate wages and benefits, and acts as a sounding board as the head of staff weighs various management decisions. Personnel committees work best when they evaluate clergy but leave the evaluation of the rest of the staff to the head of staff.

If possible, people who serve on personnel committees in congregations should be individuals who have personnel management responsibilities in their secular lives. The committee needs to represent the diversity of the congregation as a whole. However, problems will develop if members of the committee are chosen because they represent various constituencies within the congregation. Staff will become pawns in the battles between competing constituencies.

One key is to avoid committees or boards thinking they are responsible for managing the entire staff. When I first came to Western, the congregation had been through a series of interim-type pastors. With a constant flow of short-term pastorates, the board of trustees ended up managing our building-cleaning-and-maintenance person. During that tumultuous time, there was no consistent management from the board or its president; management took place according to the whims or availability of the trustees. The scars on our building person from that period of mismanagement-by-committee took a long time to heal.

In general, management of individuals by groups is a disaster. When committees or members of the congregation are allowed to manage paid staff, the result is either high staff turnover or angry staff. Indeed, one of the key functions of top management in a congregation is to make sure that management of the staff remains within the staff. As head of staff, one of my responsibilities is to communicate clearly and firmly to a few wannabe managers among our membership that I have the staff management responsibility under control.

While this may sound a bit hierarchical, it does not have to be hierarchical in practice. Yes, there is a clear line of responsibility and accountability. However, a good manager pulls a staff together into a goal-oriented team whose decisions become collaborative. As decisions, accomplishments, and failures are shared, the vertical flow chart of responsibility becomes and feels horizontal in practice.

In summary, it is crucial to have clear understandings regarding who is managing whom within a congregation's personnel system. Committees supply important feedback to clergy as to how they are performing. It is the head of staff's responsibility to manage the rest of the staff, making sure they feel they are part of a productive team, successfully achieving the larger goals of the congregation's mission.

Managing Personnel as Parts of a System

Systems theory is a powerful tool in the management of personnel. The biggest problem in personnel is that managers tend to treat individual employees differently. Certainly every person is an individual and needs to be respected as such. However, every person expresses his or her individuality within the context of systems: family systems, cultural systems, and work systems. An effective manager considers each staff member both as a unique individual and as part of a system.

My wife was a teacher in the D.C. public schools for more than thirty years. Like every other teacher in the system, she received an annual *individual* performance evaluation—rating her on everything from the appearance of her classroom to the quality of classroom discussions. But to what end? How did this performance evaluation improve the functioning of the school system? Many of the problems limiting my wife's ability to bring out the best in her students were systemic. The copying machine rarely had paper, computers were archaic or nonexistent, printers were out of ink, textbooks were rarely available during the first month of classes, and students sometimes hadn't received proper training for her literature class in their preceding courses. Evaluations of each teacher's individual performance did little to create a system where children received the education they wanted and deserved. Being evaluated as an individual in a dysfunctional system was also an alienating experience for high quality teachers who knew they weren't the problem. Just as bad, it allowed ineffective teachers to blame the system rather than holding themselves accountable for their own shortcomings.

Individual performance evaluations can be a bit like evaluating the tires on a car that needs a new motor. So what if the car has good or bad tires? Unless the other systemic issues are resolved, the performance of the tires is irrelevant.

Aligning Staff toward Congregational Goals

For fifteen years, Jane had been the secretary at All Souls Church, a congregation of 200 members. She was a remarkably competent person who served the congregation well, and church members loved her. During her time at All Souls, the congregation's membership was relatively stable, but the pastor's office had a revolving door. Jane worked with four heads of staff. The congregation came to see themselves and Jane as the stable factors in the congregational system while the clergy were the variable factor. Jane was well aware of this reality.

When Harold, the latest new pastor, arrived at All Souls, he was determined to help the congregation grow in membership. But it was clear to Jane that Harold had little attachment to All Souls. Indeed, he came right out and told Jane he didn't intend to stay long. He was interested in growing All Souls so he could move on to something bigger and better. As Harold saw it, it was a win-win for him and All Souls.

To create a climate for growth rather than continuing the existing climate for maintenance, Harold instituted a number of changes. Almost every change involved more work for Jane. Given the current size of the congregation, there was no possibility of hiring additional office help or increasing Jane's salary significantly.

While Harold became famous for brief, drive-by encounters with All Souls' members, Jane had weekly contact with various key congregational leaders. They called her for advice on things like scheduling meetings or involving members in their pet projects. At the end of each call, almost invariably, members asked her, "So Jane, how do you like Harold? How is he doing?" With her closest friends in the congregation, Jane was honest about her feelings that the new pastor was overloading her with work and felt no lasting commitment to All Souls. Within a year of his arrival at All Souls, Harold approached the chair of the personnel committee and said he needed to replace Jane. "She is undermining everything I am trying to do."

Many congregations and clergy would view this situation as a classic personality clash—a simple case of two individuals who don't get along. However, the problem is rooted in the system. A significant portion of the system didn't want to change (grow), and Jane was symbolic of that reluctance to change. Another part of the system wanted to change (especially the folks who hired Harold after they heard his growth agenda) and viewed Harold's success as symbolic of the ability to create change and growth. Unless the systemic issues are confronted and clarified, bringing in a new secretary or a new pastor won't solve the problem. Nor will changing the job descriptions, improving personnel evaluations, hiring additional staff, or giving raises.

Using a strategic planning process, the congregation needs to determine its goals. One central question for this church is whether it wants to grow or stay the same. Once the congregation has a sense of its goals, it needs to create a staffing plan with individuals who are committed to reaching the goals and then, through good management, have them work toward the goals. Staff members who want to remain and work on the goals should be encouraged to do so. Staff members who don't want to work on the goals should be given notice they will be let go. Perhaps performance incentives might also be considered.

Staff performance needs to be evaluated using the strategic plan as the guide. At regular intervals, it is important to measure whether the staff, committees, and leadership are effectively employing the system's strategies. Using the performance measure in the strategic plan, this determination would be made by the church governing board, head of staff, and the staff as a whole. In some instances, an outside consultant can also be helpful in this process, especially if the consultant was involved in the original planning process.

When a congregation adopts a systems approach to evaluating personnel, it recognizes that the individual can't succeed unless the system succeeds. It encourages people to work together for the good of the whole. If the system doesn't prosper, blaming the staff is not the only option (although it is one option). But perhaps the planners have an unrealistic vision, or other factors are at work in the system undermining progress. In any case, the congregation's lay leadership will need to reevaluate their plans using a systemic approach.

Let's change the scenario. Harold arrives as the new pastor with a commitment to staying at All Souls and growing the congregation. Jane's fifteen years at All Souls have revealed her to be an amiable but inefficient secretary. She is someone whom the pastor and lay leaders must work around rather than work with. Everybody is dissatisfied with Jane, but no one wants to be the "bad guy" who demands that she be replaced.

What does Jane's staying in her job for fifteen years despite a displayed lack of ability or aptitude tell us about the system? Certainly, one possibility is that the congregation avoids confrontation like the plague. Another possibility is that the congregation doesn't really want to grow, so Jane's inability to fulfill her responsibilities is irrelevant. Perhaps the congregation has never taken the time to have a thorough personnel review of Jane's performance. Whatever the conclusion, the issue isn't Jane *per se*. The system has a problem. Identifying and resolving the systemic problem(s) will lead to a solution to resolving Jane's ineffectiveness. Whether she should be fired, moved to a position where she is effective, or another alternative will be thought out in terms of the overall goals and strategies of the congregation.

It isn't surprising that congregations think about the performance of individual staff members rather than staff performance as a whole. After all, congregations function in the broader context of a highly individualistic U.S. society. In many regards this emphasis on the individual is absolutely wonderful. Citizens have amazing opportunities to express themselves and use their talents. However, when it comes to personnel issues, an individualistic approach often leads to false solutions and misidentified problems. By focusing on individuals, not systems, congregations, almost invariably, blame individuals for troubles that may in fact be more systemic.

Another example involves the classic pastor–director of music battle. Talk to the pastoral head of staff, and you'll hear one version of the problem. Talk to the music director, and you'll hear another. Typically, in these conflicts, the director of music wants one type of music while the pastor prefers a different type. Such battles usually aren't rooted in a personality conflict or even a difference of musical taste between two individuals. Rather, the conflict often boils down to a congregation allowing the two individuals to play out a difference of opinion that exists in the congregation as a whole. The congregation doesn't have the stomach to battle through its differing preferences in music, so members watch and encourage the head of staff and director of music to go at it.

To break through the deadlock, the head of staff doesn't need to fire the director of music. Rather, she needs to lead the congregation through a strategic planning process around the issue of music in worship. The process can clarify the goals of the music ministry and identify strategies to accomplish the goals. Perhaps one goal would be to have more diverse musical offerings in worship.

Are such planning processes threatening to all parties with a stake in the debate? Absolutely! This is why congregations avoid doing the planning in a formal manner. However, in planning processes, conflicts can be depersonalized, which is always less threatening than the highly personalized conflicts of which we hear so often.

Effective personnel managers frame issues in systemic rather than personal ways. Personnel performance is evaluated within the context of the strategic plan. Individual goals are aligned with the congregation's overall goals as stated in a strategic mission plan.

Of course, sometimes it is just an individual problem. I once had to fire a person who was robbing supplies from the church. There was no systemic issue that could explain his behavior. But the number of solely dysfunctional individual problems is far outnumbered by the number of cases where the problem has a systemic cause and, therefore, requires a systemic solution.

Using Teams to Manage

Over the past several decades, the concept of team has moved to the forefront in management circles. In the 1970s and 1980s when Japanese companies began to out-perform U.S. companies, great emphasis was placed on the Japanese "team" approach to organizational behavior. Many Americans believed Japanese teams gave them a huge competitive advantage. Maybe it did. Maybe it didn't. While I am convinced the use of teams can be a good thing, it can't be a "name only" change. It has to be a change in the way one thinks about and tackles opportunities and problems.

Almost anyone can grasp the team concept by sitting through a seminar or reading an article about team-building. This is what makes it so dangerous and misused. A congregation can't simply start referring to all its committees as "teams" and think it has made a change. A change in language does not necessarily indicate a change in organizational behavior. Someone once told me that institutions change the names of things as a way of lying to themselves that they are changing. How true!

St. Luke's church had a large staff working on a diverse set of ministry initiatives. When the congregation needed to replace its recently retired pastor, it made a decision to look for someone who would work to develop a sense of team. The congregation felt the previous pastor had allowed the staff to become a group of individuals who related to one another poorly and, in some instances, in ways that were counterproductive. Among the staff there were communication problems, turf battles, and unhealthy competition for resources. Most communication went vertically to the pastor with little horizontal communication among the staff itself.

After she arrived, the new pastor, Charlotte, called the staff together and introduced teamwork concepts she had used successfully in her previous call. She explained the staff would rotate leadership of the staff meetings. Within the larger staff team, there would be smaller teams devoted to Christian education, mission, and worship, each of which would have its own goals and standards of accountability. These smaller teams would include lay leadership as well as professional staff.

As might be expected, the team concept was greeted with a combination of enthusiasm and skepticism. On the one hand, staff members were tired of the hierarchical, silo-style management of the previous head of staff. On the other hand, one staff member noted, "She is still the boss whether she runs the staff meeting or one of us runs it. What has actually changed?"

After about a year with the new team approach, a major problem developed in the Christian education area. Parents were complaining that their kids didn't like the curriculum. Teachers felt they weren't being given adequate training and support. The teenagers were staying away from the youth fellowship program in droves.

As head of staff, the pastor's solution to all these complaints was to fire the director of Christian education, who headed the Christian Ed team. In her exit interview, the fired DCE said, "I thought we were working on this as a team. If I'd thought my head would roll if things went wrong, I would have run this program entirely differently. I was trying to be a team player." Other staff members who led teams began discussing their fears that they might be the next one fired. The team concept was all but dead at St. Luke's.

The team concept is not for the faint of heart. It requires an intense commitment as well as an enormous amount of additional time and work to be employed successfully. It requires a congregation and its staff to shift from solely individual to group responsibility. It is also an educational project. Staff and laity need to understand that there will be more group accountability.

When the complaints began to come in regarding the CE program, Charlotte could have sat down with the CE committee (including the director) and asked, "What are *we* doing wrong that we are getting all these complaints?" Or she might have asked the Session, "Is there something we are doing wrong as a congregational system that we don't support and promote Christian education the way our members expect? Can someone give me a brief 'family history' of the CE program in this congregation?" In either case, the team approach would have been employed rather than defaulting to an individualistic approach. This would have been management by, through, and with teams.

When I was in my Executive MBA program, the use of teams was, for many of us, perhaps the most challenging aspect of the program. Much of our work was done in teams, and on those projects we were graded as teams. At the end of the first term, a number of us complained to our teammates, "We are getting better grades in our individual work than we receive in our group projects. This group is hurting our grades!"

A dean of the business school, who happens to be a Presbyterian elder, called us together to talk through our dissatisfaction with one another as a team. He pointed out the challenges of moving from being highly individual achievers, as each of us was, to being highly individual achievers working together effectively as a team. After much discussion, we made a new commitment to the team approach.

Over the next three terms, we held one another accountable for producing quality work, rather than simply accepting each team member's work whether or not it was good. It led to some tense moments when we questioned a teammate's work. However, as a team, we learned to help one another strengthen individual work that was weak. In the process, we began to teach one another important things—and the grades from our group efforts began to match the grades we received on individual projects.

I highlight the team approach as a systemic alternative to the highly individualistic way decisions are often made and how leadership is exerted. But moving to a team approach is not a fix-all solution to personnel problems. It simply puts them in a different context. The individual remains responsible but within the context of the team. It is the team's job to get the job done—and individuals are evaluated based on their efforts toward that goal.

Certainly, a congregation can choose to stay in a more conventional, nonteam approach to work and management. Yet even churches that eschew the team approach need to evaluate and manage the work of individuals within the context of the larger system in which the work is done. To not do so is to focus solely on the parts and risk missing issues related to the whole. If congregations break down the hyperindividualism that plagues our culture, they will discover a shared sense of where they are going and work together to get there. It will allow congregational leadership to emerge in informal rather than formal ways.

While thinking systemically requires a lot more thought and effort than functioning as a group of individuals, the productivity and effectiveness of a congregation's ministry will be greatly enhanced by using a systems approach. Problems will be diagnosed more accurately. Opportunities will be engaged more effectively, organized better, and managed more appropriately.

Managing through Personnel Policies

As a head of staff, I rarely have to consult our personnel policies. Why? Because we have them! Personnel policies are the framework in which the management of personnel takes place. They define vacation and leave time, health and pension benefits, and sabbatical and termination policies. When employees are clear about these issues from the beginning and policies are fairly administered, a number of potentially conflictive issues are eliminated. Everyone on the staff knows what he or she is due and not due as an employee.

Rather than offering a category-by-category description of things that need to be in a congregation's personnel policies here, I have included, at the end of this chapter, a "Checklist for Personnel Committees" that includes some major things a thorough and just personnel policy needs to address. In this section I will focus my thoughts on personnel on the following areas: creating personnel policies, hiring and firing staff, compensation, job descriptions, evaluation, and creating staff stability.

CREATING PERSONNEL POLICIES

Constructing personnel policies is time-intensive and inevitably produces some differences of opinion. Since such policies are normally created by a congregation's personnel committee, the first step is to form such a committee, if it does not exist already.

Getting personnel policies as templates from other congregations is the second step. In addition to reviewing the policies of other churches, you should take a look at the personnel policies from several businesses, as well. Too often, congregations fail to consider important issues that are taken for granted in the business world. For example, the policies of many congregations don't address family leave or the process for handling sexual misconduct. A personnel committee can ask congregational members to submit various personnel policies from companies where they work. The nonprofit community is another good source of personnel policy templates.

Recently, our congregation at Western reviewed our family-leave policy. Our survey of several other congregations found a wide discrepancy in how they deal with this area. We asked church members to submit policies from the secular world and, again, found huge differences among benefits offered to employees. The subject created much more debate than I expected. It would be easy to say the differences of opinion were generational—and they were, to some extent. But the opinions of the committee members also reflected the benefits they received in their secular workplaces. Some younger and older members felt church staff shouldn't be entitled to things they didn't receive in the secular workplace. But other younger and older members felt the church should be more generous than the secular workplace. Some committee members argued for longer leave time when an employee had a birth. Others felt our generous amount of vacation time should be factored into the equation, resulting in a more limited time specifically for family leave.

As usually happens in such matters, the committee reached a compromise that seems to have satisfied most people. But the process reminded me again that the church is not only a system itself. It functions within a larger system: the broader economy. We cannot expect to establish church policies in a vacuum. A congregation's policies on things like salaries, benefits, and leave will all be judged, in part, in comparison with what church members experience in their workplaces. While clergy may think their salaries are too low, what about the salaries of church members who are social workers, teachers, and auto mechanics—all highly skilled professions? Given that some clergy are paid more than members of their congregation working in these professions, these church members may well view clergy salaries and benefits as more than fair.

While creating personnel policies, compensation and benefit guidelines, and other key criteria very important to staff, it is important for the personnel committee and governing board to engage the congregation in these policies. The congregation needs to understand the logic behind the policies as well as the salaries and benefits other congregations offer staff. A personnel committee also needs to describe any denominational policies that may come into play (such as minimum salaries, vacation, or sabbaticals). This will help minimize the griping in the parking lot about these issues.

Most important, the congregation needs to be included in the process of creating new personnel policies or reevaluating existing policies, not simply handed a set of completed policies. Announcements in the church newsletter, on its website, and in worship are appropriate. As the process proceeds, requests can be made for specific types of input such as policies used in the workplaces of members. To build congregational ownership of policies as the review process comes to an end, the personnel committee can organize small group opportunities to explain the values behind the policies they are recommending. For example, they might explain that a congregation constantly preaching about the importance of the family needs a family leave policy that puts into practice what they preach. If staff members will be paid relatively low salaries, what are the values behind such a decision? What values inform vacation and sabbatical policies?

Not everyone will agree with the specifics of every personnel policy. Some people will be jealous that church staff gets better benefits than they receive at their workplaces. Others will think the church is being cheap toward its staff. However, a good personnel policy creates the framework for a healthy, ongoing debate about how employees are treated by a congregation.

JOB DESCRIPTIONS

In addition to lacking comprehensive personnel policies, too many congregations are without another basic personnel tool: job descriptions for each employee. Granted, it is challenging to create job descriptions. In the church, roles often blend. I do almost as much setting up of chairs and tables for meetings as our janitor does. The janitor does a significant amount of what I would describe as pastoral counseling. Our secretary makes a lot of decisions that are reserved for the head of staff in other congregations. However, despite the work areas where roles merge—or maybe precisely because they so often merge—job descriptions are necessary. Without them, the challenge of managing personnel becomes even more difficult.

I confess that I have not been good about creating an up-to-date job description for our janitor here at Western who has been with us for 45 years. He does what he does—and isn't going to do what he isn't going to do. Several times I've tried to work on a job description with him. It created a lot of irritation between us without much positive change. Nonetheless, both he and I will retire in the foreseeable future. There needs to be a good description for both positions. Otherwise, when Western selects a new pastor and building person, it will be guessing at what we did and did not do.

The job descriptions for clergy tend to be well established at most churches. Congregations create these whenever they have to search for a new pastor. However, the job descriptions for other staff are often defined less clearly, and can turn into laundry lists that seem endless. One way our church avoids the laundry list approach is by framing all job descriptions within the broader context of a congregation's strategic plan. Of course, to do this, a church must have a strategic plan! If a congregation doesn't have such a plan, it needs to create one. If we don't know where we are going, we'll never know when we get there.

For example, one of our goals is to build a strong, internal sense of community. Much of what our secretary does falls under this goal. Her time on the phone answering questions, stopping work to chat with members as they pass through the building, scheduling events, and making sure the space is ready for them are all things that help create a strong community.

The same is true with the janitor, who spends a significant amount of time shooting the breeze with members. When I first came to Western, this really irritated me. It felt like work not being done, time wasted. But as years passed, I realized how much ministry was being done in and through Gaston's conversations with members. I soon realized Gaston was a major weaver of the fabric of our community. I would put "talking with members" at the top of his job description under "Building Community."

Western also is focused on building a strong Christian education program. Both the secretary and janitor perform tasks that are crucial for this goal to be realized. All of those responsibilities can be listed under "Christian Education" in their job descriptions. Similarly, everything from creating worship bulletins, to having the sanctuary clean, to having all the light bulbs working can be placed under the goal of "Enhancing Worship" with the appropriate personnel.

There is a real advantage to creating job descriptions that link up with a congregation's strategic plan. To illustrate what it might look like, I have related a few work tasks to a congregation's goals in the chart on the next page.

Using this methodology, each staff member can see how his or her work is advancing the overall mission of the congregation. Each person's work input is identified with very specific ministry output. A janitor is no longer just setting up the chairs for a class. He is helping us build a strong education program. The church secretary is no longer cranking out a bulletin. She is creating an absolutely essential aid to an inspiring, enriching worship experience.

Finally, job descriptions are often created in preparation for hiring a new staff person. While this is necessary, it is equally important to make adjustments to the descriptions once a new person has been on the job for a year or so. No one does everything well; but most people can do a few things very well. Job descriptions can be reworked to highlight employees' strengths. Alternate arrangements can be made to get other work done. Obviously, if the primary accompanist isn't a good musician, a congregation may not be able to work around that problem. But with creative thinking and reworked job descriptions, it is possible to maximize staff members' strengths and minimize exposing their weaknesses. This approach reminds us again of Paul's image of the body of Christ where each part is essential to the working of the overall body.

Goals from Congregation's Strategic Plan:	Job Description: Pastor	Job Description: Secretary	Job Description: Janitor	Job Description: Christian Education Director	Job Description: Music Director
1. Build a strong sense of belonging to the Western community.	• Visit members in their homes. • Demonstrate responsive pastoral care. • Design retreats.	• Answer phones. • Schedule events, manage church calendar. • Chat warmly with people who come into the office and on the phone.	• Talk with members as they park in the garage. • Relate to members while setting up for events.	• Be heavily involved in the lives of our parents and children.	• Organize social events for the choir. • Organize special events around Christmas.
2. Have a Christian education that challenges members to grow spiritually.	• Teach classes periodically. • Supervise the DCE.	• Place supplies and curriculum orders for the DCE. • Place announcements about CE events in the appropriate places.	• Set up classrooms. • Know the names of kids and their parents.	• Run the CE program under the leadership of the CE committee and head of staff.	• Find ways to educate the congregation about the musical choices that are made for worship.
3. Have inspiring worship experiences.	• Organize the worship experience. • Preach inspiring sermons.	• Prepare weekly worship bulletin.	• Clean the sanctuary.	• Ensure the sound, HVAC, and other systems are working.	• Have a high quality musical presentation every Sunday.
4. Have a strong mission to the world.	• Be active in community organizations. • Lead the congregation to new mission possibilities.	• Place announcements about mission opportunities in the appropriate places.	• Prepare areas for special mission fairs.	• Link what is happening in classrooms to what is happening in the mission committee.	• Select music that includes mission themes and is multicultural.

FIGURE 2.2 Linking Job Descriptions to Strategic Plan

PERFORMANCE EVALUATION

Each employee's work should be evaluated by the person in the management scheme who is most informed. Therefore, managers are usually best positioned to evaluate the employees they manage. When personnel committees evaluate the work of staff members, they are evaluating work about which they often know precious little. Some personnel committees want to see the evaluations managers make of employees; others do not.

In the case of a head of staff, the full congregation or its governing board typically makes decisions regarding hiring and termination. However, that larger group should assign responsibility for evaluating and supporting the clergy to a personnel committee. A small personnel committee, acting with rules of confidentiality, can be extremely helpful to pastors and the congregations they serve. Conducting annual evaluations of the pastor is a primary responsibility of the personnel committee. These evaluations provide crucial feedback to pastors about their job performance. Where clergy performance is excellent, praise God. If performance is poor or needs improvement, the committee can recommend remedial steps, help the pastor set goals for the year ahead, or suggest the pastor might move to a call that better fits his or her strengths. While the latter suggestion might not be well received, it is better for the option to be discussed with a small, informed group than at a congregational meeting.

A chart like the one on page 58, which links employee job descriptions and responsibilities to strategic goals, objectives, and strategies, can be a valuable evaluation tool. This helps employees see how their work is tied to the success of the congregation and changes the nature of the evaluation in a very positive way. If a worship bulletin is filled with mistakes, it is not a conversation about proofreading but about how a mistake-filled bulletin harms the worship experience. It is not about a personal thing between an employee and me but about the effectiveness of our work together in ministry. Put in this larger framework, it is easier for the supervisor and employee to see the importance of each issue.

In our litigious times, it is important to create a written form of all evaluations. The written evaluations don't need to be long and extremely detailed, especially if an employee is performing well. They need to be placed in a locked file. Without a paper trail, it is hard either to argue for a significant jump in compensation or fire an employee. Because personnel management is about relationships, it is also important to have face-to-face conversations between supervisors and employees regarding any written evaluations. This allows both parties to share their reactions and provides an opportunity for the written evaluation to be changed, if need be.

At Western, the personnel committee has asked me, as head of staff, to perform the evaluations of part-time directors of music and education and cleaning person as well as our full-time secretary and janitor. The personnel committee conducts the evaluations of both my clergy colleague and me. I appreciate this division of labor because, frankly, few committee members are around enough to make an intelligent evaluation of every staff member's performance.

HIRING AND FIRING

Hiring staff members is one of the most important managerial decisions. If the right person is hired, the new employee's gifts can take the congregation's ministry to a higher level. But if the wrong person is hired, fixing that mistake can be a nightmare.

Firing an employee is painful, even in a secular organization not dominated by the values the church espouses. Church members want their congregation to be a place of warmth and love. Firings don't fit neatly into such a vision. The difficult decision to let someone go becomes even more painful because some members inevitably take the side of the dysfunctional employee. Furthermore, in a congregation with dysfunctional behavior, the firing will become symbolic. Members displeased with the head of staff will take the firing as evidence the head of staff is inherently unfair. Members who never wanted a staff person hired in the first place will feel vindicated. The possible scenarios are legion. So when we hire someone, if at all possible, we need to get it right.

When hiring, it is extremely important to go beyond references. What potential employee lists references who will give future employers the full scoop? Not many. Most of us list references who will say nothing but nice things about us. Worse, some references may be actively trying to get rid of the person whom they are recommending. For years, denominational executives have passed along people who were guilty of sexual misconduct or simple incompetence. To get out of this self-serving circle of references, we need to ask prospective employees for permission to speak with people who know them in a work setting. We then need to find individuals who have worked with the applicant and whose opinions we can trust. Without independent third-party advice, we may simply be hiring a person whom someone else wants to pass along. Yes, some people fear lawsuits or personal accusations if they speak the truth about a potential employee's abilities. However, there is always someone who will speak the truth. Find that person.

Personally, when it comes to hiring, I've learned not to trust in my own opinion alone. I tend to like people who don't necessarily turn out to be good employees. Therefore, to help make hiring decisions, I find congregational members with knowledge about the area in which the new person will work. For example, when we hire a secretary, I recruit from our congregation secretaries or people who supervise secretaries to help me make the decision. Using this system, I have had only one less than desirable hire.

There is no such thing as a perfect record in personnel decisions! But I believe that checking a prospective employee's background as thoroughly as possible, including people knowledgeable with the work area, and moving as expeditiously as possible are all important.

When it comes to firings, unless an employee has committed a criminal act, a paper trail regarding his or her bad performance needs to be in place. Over the course of the person's employment, the manager must meet with the employee periodically to discuss the poor performance. At the conclusion of each meeting, the manager should create a dated memo detailing the conversation. Prior to dismissal, it is generally proper to give an employee a warning.

Perhaps the person should be placed on probation, if that is an official status in a congregation's employment practices. The more detailed a congregation's personnel policies are about the process of managing ineffective employees the better. Encourage the personnel committee to devote a section of its employee policies to defining the process of dismissal. A well-defined policy guides and informs both managers and employees.

Once a decision to dismiss is made, it is necessary to consider issues such as the employee's access to computer systems and the church building. There is no need to act like some ruthless corporate employers in this regard. However, a manager does have a responsibility to protect the congregation from any destructive acts.

I will close this section by adding that the fact that congregations are exempt from many secular personnel laws does not mean we are exempt from God's laws. Our practices in hiring and firing should reflect our commitment to Jesus, the head of this body known as the church. For me, this involves treating employees the way we want to be treated. In Luke 6:31 Jesus lays out a very basic strategy for working with and managing others, "Do to others as you would have them do to you."

COMPENSATION

True, congregations are unique places of employment. Our goal is faithfulness, not profit. There are tremendous benefits flowing from the, hopefully, God-aligned work we do. In my opinion, these benefits far outweigh the salaries paid in some other vocations. However, the many benefits are no excuse for underpaying our church employees.

Like many congregations, Western offers certain benefits the secular world doesn't offer. Our secretary, Shenella McGaskey, made much more money in her previous job at a law office. However, she feels called to work in the church. That said, she is not going to sacrifice her family's well-being by working for a pauper's wages. Therefore, we put together a decent salary, good benefits, and a meaningful job to convince her to work with us. Combine the joy and satisfaction that flows from ministry work with a decent compensation package and the church can compete with secular businesses in hiring talented women and men.

There are easy ways to find the going, competitive salaries for various spots on a staff. When it comes to janitors and secretaries, the competitive rates are in the secular world. It is important to know what people are being paid in the communities where we seek to hire someone. This is a perfect place to put the personnel committee to work. Committee members can seek out what people are being paid for various types of work in their and other workplaces. There is also a lot of salary information online.

Another interesting but challenging task for a personnel committee is to think through and record why different positions are compensated differently. Does the senior pastor make significantly more than an associate pastor? If so, why? There are good answers to the question. However, if the answers are not understood, associate pastors will feel undervalued. The supporters of associate pastors will also be upset. If a congregation has a well-thought-out rationale for its compensation scheme, it may head off some of the grumbling around this issue that takes place in many churches.

HIRING AND COMPENSATING CLERGY

When it comes to clergy, many denominations have minimum salary and benefit packages. There are many factors that go into creating a salary and benefit package including regional housing prices, costs of living, and job markets. Reflecting the high cost of living in the Washington, D.C. metro area, our National Capital Presbytery has a relatively high minimum salary. One way to evaluate the fairness and competitiveness of church salaries is to compare them with secular salaries that demand comparable education and workloads. Salaries in the church don't have to equal those in the secular world. However, secular salaries can be used as a benchmark by which compensation decisions in the church are justified.

For example, our Presbytery's minimum salary is about $20,000 higher than the average salary of social workers in our region who have master's degrees. This would argue for the Presbytery to have a lower minimum salary. However, social workers have real difficulty living in this region on their salaries. So a higher minimum for the Presbytery makes sense. While our Presbytery minimum allows a single person to live in our region, it certainly does not enable them to buy a home or condo. Given the high cost of living in the Washington, D.C. metro area, even our Presbytery's high minimum salary is less than attractive to many potential candidates for open pastoral positions here.

Working off judicatory minimum salary rules is not always a good place to start when pricing a staff position. A congregation needs to evaluate what other local congregations are paying, what it costs to live in the region, and how much more the church is willing to pay for someone with more ministry experience. With that key data, a congregation should be able to establish a salary range for a position that is both just and competitive.

One consideration in establishing salary ranges is the amount of flexibility the employee is given to pursue other interests—either within or outside the church. If a person is expected to put in 50–60 hour workweeks, he or she should be well compensated for that time commitment. The employee's job is basically going to be his or her life. If the staff member is expected to work 40 hours a week or less, that might be reason for a lower compensation package. Personally, I consider my generous vacation and study leave allowances to be worth a lot of cash. I'd rather have a lower salary and better leave benefits than vice versa.

Given the high housing costs in the Washington, D.C. and many other areas, clergy housing expenses are a major issue. In what is increasingly becoming standard practice, Western entered a share-equity agreement with our associate pastor so she could find a home close enough to the church to make the commute reasonable. (An unreasonable commute will limit a pastor's availability to the congregation and quickly erode his or her effectiveness.) Other congregations have given favorable loans to staff members so they can buy houses. The use of a manse or parsonage seems to be reemerging as a popular housing option.

Let me offer one additional word about the hiring of clergy. Although many denominations have an established process that defines the length of the interim between pastors, I'm not convinced a long interim pastorate is always healthy.[1] In my experience long interims (more than 6–12 months) are usually not times of healing but rather times of drift and demoralization. While many churches and denominations are sold on the interim process, I know of no other organization that waits so long to replace key personnel. The rationale for this delay is that the clergy-congregation relationship is unique—and this is certainly true. But the same could be said of many other employee-employer relationships. The relationship between a company and its founder is unique. But when the founder retires, a company doesn't wait 12–24 months to replace the executive. The relationship between a nonprofit community service organization and its director is unique. However, a nonprofit waits more than several months to replace the founder at its own peril. The church needs to stop seeing itself as more unique than we are. If it does, congregations will speed up the process by which clergy openings are filled.

APPEALS

As a congregation creates personnel policies and practices, one key concern is dispute resolution. What happens if someone feels he or she is being treated unfairly? To me, it has always seemed patently unfair that a church employee usually has no appeal beyond the head of staff. Well-managed businesses have defined appeal processes that preserve the chain of command while not turning managers into dictators. There is no reason a congregation cannot do the same.

An appeal process has to be well defined so employees know how and when they can appeal the head of staff's decision. Churches don't want a system where employees can take every concern to the personnel committee, feeling they don't need to deal with the head of staff. However, even the best boss can be unfair, at times, so every employee should be explicitly informed of the appeal process. The personnel committee has to be wise in handling appeals to insure that the head of staff's authority is not undermined.

As a manager, I couldn't do my job without occasionally being able to say to a staff member, "Okay, if you don't like my decision, here is what you can do. You can talk to the personnel committee." I haven't had to do it often. But it has been a lifesaver when I have done it. The appeals usually concerned what was considered a reasonable workload. I had one expectation; the staff member had another expectation. In these situations, I welcomed the mediation of the personnel committee.

KEEPING GOOD STAFF IN PLACE

If a congregation establishes and employs good personnel policies and practices—regarding everything from hiring to compensation to helpful options for housing to flexible work hours—it should be able to retain quality staff. This is incredibly important in building a ministry. The amount of time and energy that goes into finding good staff and helping new staff integrate into a congregation is enormous. When a staff stays in place, all that time and energy can go into the ministry itself. Prospective new members usually are attracted to a congregation, in part, by the staff. With a stable staff, they can be assured the existing staff will stay in place if they join.

Furthermore, congregations are like families. Understanding how the family functions, which family members need attention, which can be difficult—these are things we learn over time as we serve a congregation. When a staff member leaves, all that information about the family goes with him or her. It has to be relearned by the next staff person.

When studying best practices in business, I found that good companies also view their employees as family. General Electric, for example, has a long history of hiring from within. They spend a lot of time developing employees through training, giving them the skill sets they need, and helping them become comfortable with GE's corporate culture. By keeping employees, GE discovered that keeping a leader slotted in a managerial position will, over a period of time, cause that person to lose his or her risk-taking leadership tendencies. As a result, when they identify members of their corporate family as leaders, they move them around and up. Would that the church family would do the same with its young leaders!

I consider staff retention to be a key reason our congregation has grown. In my twenty-five years at Western, we have had one head of staff, two part-time directors of music, two associate pastors (the position was created fifteen years ago), one janitor, and about six secretaries (it took us a while to find the right one!). I can't count the number of times potential new members have asked me, "Are you planning on leaving any time soon? What about the associate pastor and director of music?" The staff is one of their reasons for joining. As a result, new members want to ensure continuity of staffing is a value at Western.

Continuity of staff also means that we know one another. Within our staff, we happen to like one another. But even if we didn't, we know pretty much how the other person is going to respond to a new idea. In worship, when we make mistakes, the other members of the liturgical leadership team have been around long enough to know how to cover for the error.

I am definitely in the "employee you know is better than the one you don't" camp. I would much rather try to work with staff members I know well—making use of their strengths and working through or around their weaknesses—than constantly bring in new people whose strengths and weaknesses I don't know. To that end, I think forcing a rigid job description on an employee is a huge mistake. When hiring, there needs to be a job description. However, as I stated above, the head of staff and congregation need to be open to changing a staff person's job description as the gifts the new employee brings to the job become more evident. What if the new staff member is a great preacher? Will the job description still read, "Preach every six weeks"? That seems like a huge waste of talent. What if the person is a fabulous administrator? Does the administration responsibility still need to fall exclusively with the head of staff?

Managing a staff is far more than creating job descriptions to meet the needs of the ministry. It is a fascinating puzzle to solve.

We need to fit staff people together in our ministry in a way that maximizes their skills and minimizes their weaknesses. This is what teamwork is all about. I always tell people that one reason I have stayed at Western for twenty-five years is the way the congregation brings out my strengths and hides my weaknesses. They don't want me doing tasks I do poorly, and they relish the things I do well. Of such is the chemistry of a long-term pastorate!

Personnel management requires a mindset more than a particular personality. When a head of staff is managing to a specific strategic plan, with good personnel policies in place and a clear understanding of the congregational and surrounding societal systems, he or she has an excellent chance of success and the congregation increases its chances of achieving its desired outputs—proclamation, pastoral care, programs, and mission. Therefore, as we manage, we need to create the structure needed to maximize the "people" input required for successful ministry outputs.

Manager's Checklist

- What theological and biblical values inform your congregation's personnel policies and management?
- Does your congregation have a strategic plan? Are personnel policies, evaluations, and decisions linked directly to the plan? Is it clear who is managing whom? If not, why not? (Applying a systemic analysis to this question may lead to surprising and helpful answers.) Is the pastoral staff's performance linked in evaluations to the strategic plan's goals?
- What would it mean for your staff and congregation to employ a team approach to work?

Checklist for Personnel Committees

- If a personnel committee does not already exist, the congregation should create one, seeking out individuals who are knowledgeable about personnel matters and trusted by the congregation and staff.

- Have the committee gather personnel policies from other churches in the region to use as templates for creating or revising the congregation's policies. Research denominational resources and mandates for personnel.
- Identify the key issues personnel policies need to address such as parental leave, sabbatical policies, sick and personal leave (does it carry over from year to year?), and the various benefits provided for full-time and part-time employees.
- In a multiple clergy staff, think through the rationale for the salary and benefits offered to different pastors. If all pastors are paid the same, why? If different pastors make different salaries, what is the rationale for this (longevity with the congregation or denomination, more responsibility, etc.)?
- Check with denominational sources for any guidelines or mandates as well as for any governmental mandates.
- Recommend the new or revised personnel policy to the congregation's governing board with accompanying rationales for the various concepts and values in the policy.
- Before final approval, run the policies by the staff for comment (not for a vote but for comment).

chapter 3

Managing Facilities

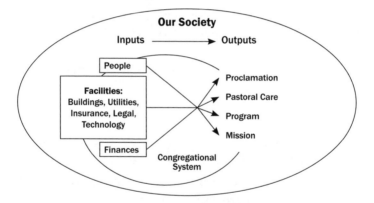

FIGURE 3.1 Facilities Inputs

W hile managing, effective pastors recognize the interdependence and interaction between a system's parts
and the whole. They also understand the connections between three basic systemic inputs—people,
facilities, and finances—required to achieve desired
ministry outputs. Use of a systems approach illuminates how managing a congregation's facility, including its technological assets,
can be key in helping that church achieve its goals in ministry.

The International Facility Management Association offers a helpful definition that emphasizes the systemic nature of the task: "Facility management is a profession that encompasses multiple disciplines to ensure functionality of the built environment by integrating people, place, process, and technology."[1] In fact, there is no other part of congregational management in which the systems approach is more obvious than when handling facilities. When the electrical system isn't functioning, not much else in the system works. When something breaks down in the technology system, it cripples the ability of the staff to do things as simple as type the bulletin for worship or check e-mail.

Congregations use their buildings to worship God, feed the hungry, educate their members and children, and organize their communities for justice and compassion. Increasingly, they use technology for that most important task in ministry—communication. If a congregation allows its facilities to deteriorate and become unsafe, it can hinder that church's entire ministry.

For example, in 1994, Western built a new facility in the Foggy Bottom neighborhood where our church has been in ministry since 1855. The primary reason for the move was the congregation's failure to maintain the building it constructed in 1930. Because of a lack of money, it had allowed the old building's systems to deteriorate. For the first decade of my ministry at Western, much of my time went into damage control regarding the physical condition of the old building. The costs of repairing the outdated facility were overwhelming. It didn't have to be that way.

Managing buildings and technology does not have to be a huge drain on the time of a pastor or members. However, failing to manage buildings and technology will create problems that consume incredible amounts of time and money. For example, the shutdown of a congregation's server or Internet service can almost bring the work of the staff to a halt. Bad management in these areas also generates great anxiety within the congregational system. If facilities management is framed within the context of what a congregation is accomplishing for God, the work can be extremely meaningful. The many details of management are given greater purpose when seen as part of the congregation's mission.

Fundamentally, facilities management boils down to two key components: personnel and money. Surely, finding and keeping good personnel is a challenge. However, there are lots of good folks out there looking for work. If building personnel are understood as members of the congregational family, treated and compensated fairly, and helped to view their work as contributing to the well-being of the congregational system, they are much more likely to be committed long-time employees.

Money is money. Either a congregation has it or it doesn't. When a congregation has very limited financial resources to apply to facilities, wise and effective management becomes even more important.

Congregations that delay building maintenance end up with a dirty and unsafe building. This is a very big deal for several reasons. First, an unsafe building is morally indefensible. People can get hurt or even die as a result of inadequate maintenance. Second, the state of the church building is an important evangelism issue. A visitor or potential new member often sees the parking lot and building before meeting any member of the congregation or its staff. The state of the facilities is a major statement about the congregation's health. If the parking lot is in bad shape, visitors will expect to find things in bad repair within the building. If a congregation's technology is outdated, younger potential members are sure to take note. If a church's nursery or childcare facilities are not safe and clean, families with children simply aren't going to join the church.

Whether large or small, well endowed or struggling financially, every congregation needs to find a way to take care of its facilities. It really isn't helpful to get into the mission versus building maintenance debate. As I learned when we had a debate over establishing a capital reserve fund at Western, it is a false choice. If a congregation is going to continue in its mission for the long haul, every generation of its members has to take care of the buildings it has inherited from a prior generation or built itself. If the current members fail in this responsibility, they will give the next generation not a building but a burden.

To better understand the task of managing a congregation's facilities, in this chapter we will:

1. understand the church building and facilities as input systems in need of being managed as such;
2. recognize the importance of personnel, funding maintenance, monitoring costs of utilities and insurance, securing and maintaining desired technology for ministry, and making sure all possible legal issues are addressed responsibly;
3. clarify the role of the trustees or facilities committee.

Facilities Management from a Systems Perspective

If a congregation has the original architectural and construction drawings for the church building, something very important can be seen. There isn't just one set of blueprints. The average person associates blueprints with the layout of a building. However, there are also blueprints for the foundation, steel/structural support system, electrical and technology wiring, plumbing, landscaping, water management, and other facets of the building. Each set of blueprints represents a system within a system.

When managing a building, in order to understand how things fit together, it is necessary to consider each system (mechanical, electrical, etc.) within the larger system of the overall building. For example, recently at Western, a vandal ripped out an entry-door release panel for the building's garage door. The panel allows people at the garage entrance to buzz an office so someone there can open the door remotely. What seemed like a simple repair turned out to be a nightmare because of all the different building systems involved in opening the garage door.

First, we discovered that simply replacing the vandalized entry panel in our fourteen-year-old security system wasn't an option. In the world of security technology, the entry panel was a dinosaur. Since the system was old, it needed old parts—old parts that were no longer available. Once we installed a new master panel, all the intercoms had to be replaced because they were not compatible with the new panel.

Second, the security folks needed to run a new cable, with more capacity for information, outside to the new panel. This involved digging through an area of landscaping that contained an irrigation system and gas line.

Third, after the new panel was installed, the control on the garage door kept shorting out. Each time there was a short, the door opened. We had to involve the door maintenance company and an electrician to solve that issue before the new panel would function properly.

Therefore, an expense that looked reasonable at first became enormous. In order to replace the entry panel, we had to replace the master panel for the entire system, install a new door opener, run new cable, and replace the intercoms—at a cost of more than $20,000.

By the way, we also replaced the vendor. Some companies install proprietary equipment for various major systems. If the system is proprietary, all service and parts must be provided by the company that did the installation—because no other companies sell the parts. Faced with what amounted to an entirely new system, we chose a different vendor who does not install proprietary equipment. The parts are available from multiple sources. If the congregation is ever dissatisfied with the new company's work, there are numerous other companies in the D.C. area that can service the system.

This example reveals the importance of thinking systemically. In facilities, few things operate in isolation from other things. Systems consist of parts. Therefore, when planning for the future, congregations need to think about the replacement and maintenance costs of entire systems. How much longer will the roofing system protect the building from the elements? Are the building's electrical panels up to code? When was the last time the fire alarm and sprinkler systems were checked? Are there HVAC filters that need to be cleaned regularly to ensure clean air? What is the cost and benefit of replacing all existing light bulbs with energy-efficient bulbs?

A congregation should know the state of readiness of all of its systems. It also helps a manager to think systemically rather than dealing with one small problem at a time. Particularly with a recurring problem, the problem may be systemic, not the more isolated repeating problem.

Building Management

The primary challenges of building management include having the right personnel to keep the building safe and clean, scheduling and funding proper maintenance (regular and major), managing utility expense, and securing adequate insurance and legal advice.

But it all begins with people. . .

PERSONNEL

As with just about everything else in ministry, if a congregation has the right people in place to care for its building, good things will happen. There are several crucial people involved in building management in most congregations: the secretary or administrative assistant, building maintenance and cleaning personnel, and the head of staff.

The Secretary
I have yet to find a church where the administrative assistant is not a key person in the building management system. First, as the keeper of the master calendar, this staff member frequently schedules events and notifies the rest of the staff what needs to be done. When setup and cleaning people don't know what's taking place in the building, they get very upset!

Second, the secretary is often a key part of the feedback loop regarding building issues. A Sunday school teacher will complain to the secretary about the temperature of a classroom. A bride will explain what she expects in the way of a waiting room prior to the ceremony. A neighbor will stop by to say the sidewalks weren't shoveled in a timely manner. The secretary often ensures that such concerns are passed along to the appropriate people to be addressed.

Third, whether they are too busy or just too self-absorbed, heads of staff regularly miss details that have enormous significance. What managers don't know, we can't fix. So all managers need multiple sets of eyes and ears to help them know what is going on in a staff, building, and congregation. For effective building management (and technology management, which we'll address later in this chapter), the secretary's input can be crucial.

Lines of authority and responsibility between the administrative assistant and the janitorial or cleaning staff must be well defined. One of my good friends was the pastor of a church where the secretary thought she was the boss of the janitorial staff. As head of staff, my friend thought he was in charge of the cleaning staff. This led to more than confusion and conflict. My colleague let the situation deteriorate to the point where the secretary quit because she thought he had undermined her authority. This, in turn, led to her friends in the congregation becoming upset with him.

When defining job roles, there are several key questions to consider:

- What kind of system is used to communicate daily use, maintenance, and cleaning of the church building? Some churches use a large daily calendar. Increasingly, that calendar is computerized—which may create problems if cleaning staff do not have access to the computer system or are not familiar with the software. Regardless of how the schedule is posted, the janitorial staff must check it regularly to stay aware of what is happening. Some churches also use message boards or mail boxes where notes can be posted with requests for actions not necessarily related to the calendar itself. Most congregations have some combination of these strategies.
- Does the secretary have authority to initiate work for the janitorial staff that is outside their regular job? If yes, what? If the cleaning and maintenance staff has not been explicitly

told they will receive direction from the secretary, it will create conflict.

- Who makes the phone calls to outside contractors requesting work: the secretary, janitorial staff, a member of the building and grounds staff, a business manager, or a pastor? If the work may be expensive, do other congregational decision-makers need to be consulted? Is there a dollar amount above which higher authority is required? ("If it costs more than $1,000, you need to check with the head of the building committee.")
- Who signs for completed work by the outside contractors? This is a big deal. When you accept the work, you commit to pay for the work. The person signing for the work needs to be qualified to judge if the work has been done well.
- Who goes over the invoices from contractors to make sure the work billed matches the work done? (This key step is often missed in churches.) The person supervising the work needs to double-check the billing invoice before it goes to the treasurer or bookkeeper, because that person probably was not involved in authorizing and monitoring the work. Too many times, contractors make honest (and not so honest) mistakes in their billing. Checking the invoices is not a time-consuming task but it can be a money-saving task. At Western, I check invoices—which also keeps me informed of what is going on in the facilities management area. It doesn't require much of my time, and ensures that I'm in the loop.
- Does the secretary have the authority to give feedback directly to the cleaning staff about its performance? I would say this should never happen. If it does, the secretary has become the acting head of staff or a member of the personnel committee.
- When the secretary's role is well defined and addresses the issues I have described, the secretary and building maintenance staff should be able to work together harmoniously. When staff have questions about responsibilities and authority, they should immediately check with the head of staff. It is easier to solve a problem before it occurs than after it has mushroomed into a major event.

Building Maintenance and Cleaning Personnel

To illustrate personnel options in the building maintenance area, let me begin by talking about two very different individuals whom I have been blessed to work with and supervise: Jim Pangle and Gaston Paige. Both Jim and Gaston have worked as the building maintenance staff for churches where I was pastor. Each had his own very personal way of going about the work, and their differences well illustrate the different approaches individuals can bring to cleaning and maintaining a building. I describe Jim as an entrepreneurial employee, and Gaston as a faithful servant. In their different ways of doing their work, these men demonstrate the need to develop a method for managing a building that matches the strengths of the personnel on a congregation's staff.

I worked with Jim Pangle as his immediate supervisor when I was an associate pastor at Bradley Hills Presbyterian Church in Bethesda, Maryland, during the late 1970s. Jim is an exceptionally bright person who could have pursued a career as a lawyer, teacher, or just about anything else. Given his intellectual curiosity, one of my goals was to keep him engaged as our primary building and maintenance staff person. I knew Jim wasn't going to stay around long if he were limited to mopping floors and replacing paper in restrooms. Jim could strip and buff floors with the best, identify preventive maintenance issues that needed attention, and think ahead about needs for upcoming meetings, classes, and worship. When there was a significant building problem, he would come to me full of suggestions about how we could solve the problem. Telling Jim what to do, in a rigid manner, would have been a surefire way to lose him as an employee. Involving him in decision-making was a way to keep him at Bradley Hills.

For me to grow as a manager, I needed to help Jim grow professionally as well, providing him with ever-new and expanding responsibilities. To that end, I asked him to take over the management of the contractors who came to fix things. He began reading up on the latest building maintenance equipment and made many suggestions regarding purchases we should make. To the degree the budget allowed, we constantly upgraded his equipment, following his recommendations.

In the end, Jim was too entrepreneurial to remain in the position at our church. Jim and his family moved to Houston, where he and his wife, Frankie, opened a cleaning service for churches, the first of its type in Houston. The Church Sexton, Inc., was an instant success and soon had more than fifty employees. By allowing Jim to explore his interests and gifts, we got four excellent years of work from him. As I see it, this is a good example of management that matches the needs of the congregation to the needs of the employee. As discussed in chapter 2, good managers find out what excites an employee and then channel the excitement in the direction of the congregation's needs.

Gaston, the faithful servant, was hired as the sexton at Western Church when he was eighteen years old. Almost fifty years later, he remains at the heart of Western's ministry. Gaston is every bit as bright as Jim. He has outstanding skills in landscaping and gardening, and does a great job contacting and supervising quality contractors for work the church needs done. He is also an exceptional ambassador to both our church members and the local community. (When he is outside gardening, he talks with lots of neighbors.) Gaston's people skills are amazing. He could have made a million dollars in sales! People talk to him about personal and professional problems they sometimes don't bring to me. Generations of Western members remember Gaston as a loving presence from their childhood days. One cannot put a price tag on what Gaston means to our congregation.

However, you may notice that I've not mentioned a few critical tasks in discussing Gaston's skill set. The building system has a few needs he isn't going to meet. For example, Gaston is not a natural handyman. To compensate, we bring in electricians and plumbers even for relatively minor repairs. And Gaston doesn't like to clean—never has, never will, and he's glad to tell you so. When he started at Western, there was a cleaning person. By the time I arrived in 1983, the Session had eliminated the position due to budgetary constraints—and the church was rarely as clean as it could have been. But as the congregation has been reborn spiritually and fiscally, we have hired a new, part-time cleaning person.

Prior to my arrival, Gaston was occasionally micromanaged by some overly controlling trustees. Worse, they tended to blame him when things went wrong. As a result, building trust between the two of us and between Gaston and church governing boards took more than a few years. It was a classic case of why I do not believe management by committee is possible. Good facilities committees work with a manager who subsequently works with employees. The committee holds the manager responsible, while the manager holds the employees and contractors responsible for cleaning and maintaining a building.

When I talk about these two wonderful men, someone inevitably asks, "Well, which one of them was better at the job?" It is a false, unnecessary choice. Both Jim and Gaston are excellent employees and I would hire either one of them in a heartbeat. Like all of us, each of them has strengths and weaknesses. The key to managing their success and job satisfaction was tailoring the job to capitalize on their strengths while covering their weaknesses by surrounding them with quality support.

When it comes to cleaning the building, many congregations employ a part-time cleaning person. For most buildings, twenty hours or less per week is sufficient time to get the job done—including floors, windows, and dusting. Finding people who do the job well is challenging, especially if the work is only part-time. Placing ads brings in all kinds of people who claim they can clean but can't. I've found word of mouth to be a better method. Let the congregation know a cleaning person is needed. Perhaps some church member employs or knows of someone who cleans homes who would be willing to come on staff and work at the church.

Outsourcing the cleaning of the church building to a quality contractor such as Jim and Frankie Pangle's The Church Sexton is another possibility. In looking for a company, a couple of questions are crucial: Do they understand the way a church's schedule impacts cleaning? Will they anticipate the needs of Sunday school teachers, choirs, and pastors? Does the company have a high turnover rate among its staff? If the answer is "yes," is there a stable manager who can assure continuity in cleaning? How does the company treat its employees and what benefits are they offered? (Most congregations want people working for them to be fairly compensated.)

Our congregation's experience with several cleaning contractors has been mixed. Companies make all kinds of promises to get the contract. In the beginning, the performance is good. However, it usually starts to slide downhill within a few months. A cleaning service can also be expensive. In the case of Jim and Frankie Pangle's company, they explain in the contract negotiations how they will save a congregation money. Because they service a large number of congregations, they get better rates on supplies. If there are any surprises, they, not the congregation, suffer the consequences. They also stress that employing their company removes the supervisory function from the pastor. Pastors are higher paid than cleaning staff. How much money does a congregation save by shifting the supervisory function from the pastor to the company? Any congregation considering this option should make the company prove its worth. Do the math.

It is important to note that most cleaning companies will not let a congregation hire any individuals employed by their cleaning staff, at least not without a steep cost. The contract usually stipulates that a congregation give the cleaning service the equivalent of six months pay in order to let their employee go to work for the church. In effect, this makes it financially unrealistic to hire the person.

Our congregation uses a building engineering service to manage the technological aspects of our relatively complex building systems. I might add that in some states, including the District of Columbia, the law requires a building to have a building engineer. Most congregations ignore the law in D.C.—but it is something to check in every jurisdiction. If the church experiences a fire, flood, or some other disaster, the lack of an engineer or engineering service might have implications for the credibility of an insurance claim.

One possibility is for a congregation to hire a certified building engineer as the primary facilities staff person. However, for many congregations, this option is too costly. Contracting with a building engineering company is another option. This is not cheap, but allowing facilities and equipment to slowly deteriorate is even more costly. A building engineering service should visit the building, at least weekly, to check the major heating, ventilation, and air conditioning systems (HVAC). They check to insure that all thermostats are set in the appropriate manner and monitor the status of vital and expensive equipment such as water heaters and electrical panels. They can usually do minor to medium size repairs for a per-incident cost.

Most building engineering services are on call 24/7. Since building problems only happen on Sunday mornings, this is quite helpful! If the heat isn't working when I arrive at church at 7:00 A.M. on Sunday morning, I call our company—and everything is usually back to normal by 9:00 A.M.

Finally, every congregation needs a comprehensive set of contractors on call for major and minor problems from inspection of elevators to pest control to vent cleaning. In the case of a crisis, usually plumbing or electrical, it is much easier to get a timely response from a contractor with whom the building manager has developed a relationship. Timely responses also directly correlate with customers who pay bills in a timely manner. One oft-forgotten contractor every church needs is someone to test fire retardant systems. Sprinklers, wall-mounted extinguishers, stove hoods, alarms, and other equipment should be checked by a professional annually. Cutting corners in this area is a big, big mistake. When our church building had a fire in 2007, our systems worked perfectly. The Fire Department said that, if the systems hadn't been properly maintained, we would have lost the entire building rather than incurring about $100,000 in damage.

The Head of Staff's Role

The pastor's role in building management will be determined by need and interest. If no one else will manage the building, the pastor has to do it. If the pastor likes to manage buildings, she or he will do it. As with all management responsibilities, it is important to define who is managing whom and what level of decisions require management to become more involved.

Building problems usually have big dollar implications. Therefore, the head of staff needs to be consulted before any expensive option is pursued. A typical chain of decision-making might look something like this:

- Below $500: The maintenance staff person makes the decision.
- $500–$2,000: The head of staff and maintenance person make the decision.
- $2,000–$5,000 or over budget: The facilities committee makes the decision.
- Over $5,000: The congregation's governing body makes the decision.

Sometimes these types of thresholds are included in a congregation's bylaws. In other situations, they are in the governing body's minutes. Regardless of where they are located, everyone on staff and in leadership needs to know them well.

Gaston comes to me, as head of staff, with various building issues for which he wants help. To the table Gaston brings the immediate issue and I bring the bigger systemic perspective, including the congregation's priorities and budget. Once we decide on a strategy, he is responsible for implementing it. I give final approval to service contracts submitted by our various contractors. Gaston makes sure the terms of the contract are fulfilled.

MANAGING FACILITIES IN TIGHT FISCAL SITUATIONS

I understand that many small congregations cannot develop an elaborate and costly web of people and services to care for and maintain the church building. When I came to Western, we had about eighty people in worship. We were a small congregation with limited financial resources. It was basically Gaston and me handling the building. We didn't have a cleaning person or building engineering service.

Given my experience in a small church, here are the key facilities management principles:

- The pastor is, by default, the building and facilities manager. This responsibility is not done well by volunteers. They may be on vacation when the roof develops a leak or busy at work when the furnace goes out. They can't manage the janitor on a daily basis. Unless there is a competent retired person to handle this responsibility, it falls on the shoulders of the pastor.
- Develop a good team. An engaged pastor, a dedicated janitor, and good, on-call contractors are the crucial core for a building-management team. (If there is a secretary, he or she is part of the team, too.) If there is no janitor, how does the building get cleaned—a cleaning service, members accepting the responsibility?
- Tend to long-term maintenance issues. Even a congregation with little money at its disposal needs to find a way to put some of its limited funds toward maintenance of the building and its systems. Ignoring important issues of building maintenance as a way of saving money is a losing strategy. The bills will only be more costly when the undermaintained systems break down.

FUNDING MAINTENANCE

Most churches fund the operations and maintenance of their building as a current expense, establishing line items in the annual operations budget for utilities, equipment, and maintenance. A few congregations also employ a strategy in which there is a capital reserve fund. As a pastor who has served churches with and without a capital reserve fund, I highly recommend that every congregation—large, small, and in-between—create one.

Examples of items financed by a capital reserve fund would include things such as replacing boilers, air handlers, roofs, and major masonry repairs. A capital reserve fund is funded through the annual operations budget. A set amount of money is transferred from the general budget to a designated account. This fund, essentially a savings account, is tapped only for a specific set of well-defined building issues. Since the money may be needed at any time, it is usually invested in very liquid forms such as money market funds or short-term treasury bills.

At Western, we have had a capital reserve fund for thirteen years. We started the fund with $150,000 taken from our endowment and currently have approximately $260,000 in the fund. We set aside $50,000 annually from our general revenues for the capital reserve fund, and have drawn on it for approximately $500,000 in major capital repairs and replacements.

The fund was created by the advocacy of one of our lay leaders, Don Allen, as he was finishing a term as president of a large nearby condominium association. He told us how they had regular assessments on condo members to keep their capital reserve fund healthy. As a result, the association didn't have huge, unexpected assessments when a roof needed replacing or some other large capital expense was needed.

Initially, I opposed the fund because I saw it as money being taken from mission for buildings. Certainly, $50,000 is a lot of money for mission! However, Don responded to my objections with very specific examples of how a capital reserve fund would protect rather than diminish our mission. He reminded us that our building is a huge part of our mission. Up to two hundred fifty homeless people rely on it daily for food and social services. About three hundred Muslims use the building for Friday prayer services. George Washington University students use the building for campus ministry. The list goes on.

In his arguments, Don was a good theologian. To pit "bricks and mortar" over and against mission, as I did initially, is being simplistic. He saw our building in incarnational terms: a fully human creation serving a fully divine purpose. In the end, Don convinced all of us to establish our capital reserve fund. It has been the blessing he predicted. When two of our air handlers failed, the $25,000 expense came straight out of the capital reserve fund. Our mission budget wasn't threatened. When we added a digital component to our organ, the $80,000 came out of the capital reserve fund. We avoided the music-versus-mission argument that plagues so many congregations.

In a small congregation with a very tight budget, such a fund may feel impossible. However, after our experience, I would argue that almost anything designated for a capital reserve fund is better than nothing. If a small congregation put aside $5,000 annually, it would be much better prepared to handle a major building problem down the line. After all, a small congregation will have a more difficult time raising money when the inevitable major building repair or replacement is required. I also think a reserve fund is a pretty easy sell to most members of a congregation. (Pastors like me are the problem!) In our personal finances, most of us keep a "rainy day" fund in case the roof on our home needs replacing, the water heater dies, or we need to buy a new automobile. Why wouldn't members want their congregation to do the same?

In determining how much to set aside annually, it is best to hire a professional to do an analysis of the building's major systems—including their health, life expectancies, and replacement costs. However, if a church can't afford such a professional assessment, members can do a reasonable estimate. The congregation's electrician, HVAC person, and plumber can give rough estimates of what will need to be replaced and when. A member can then make the phone calls required to put price tags on those items.

The goal of this analysis is to arrive at a ballpark figure for replacing the major systems and a timeframe for when the repairs will be needed. At that point, it is just math: dividing the rough estimate for total replacements by the number of years the timeframe dictates. For example, if an HVAC unit has a life expectancy of 15 years and costs $25,000, the congregation needs to be placing aside $1,700 annually. Make similar calculations for all the major systems, add them up, and a congregation will have a reasonable estimate of the annual contribution to a capital reserve fund. Again, don't get discouraged if the congregation can't save the entire amount of money needed. Get started with something.

The list of items the capital reserve fund covers can be as extensive or limited as a congregation desires. Western Church includes things such as carpeting and furniture. However, a congregation may only want to include the major HVAC systems, parking lot surfaces, and roofing. Whatever a congregation includes now won't require a fundraising drive years down the road.

In terms of stewardship and fundraising at Western, the capital reserve fund has been very helpful. I once served a congregation where continual special fundraising efforts steadily eroded the annual stewardship campaign. The congregation would have, for example, a special campaign to improve the organ, another to put on a new roof, and yet another to update the HVAC system. Members learned to hold back some money from the annual campaign so they could contribute to the inevitable special campaigns. With our capital reserve fund in place at Western, we are able to tell the congregation we will not be coming back to them later with a special fundraising drive to fund a new boiler, organ, or roof.

UTILITIES

Because utilities represent a large portion of any church budget, it is important to make sure the congregation is getting the best price possible. Recent regulatory changes mean many regions of the country now have competitive pricing. At Western, we were able to reduce our electrical costs by leaving our traditional vendor (PEPCO) and going with Washington Gas-Electric. Because our volume usage is high enough, we were eligible for a small business mass consumer rate. (Utility companies understand that congregations are small businesses even if we don't.) This change has reduced our electrical costs by 20 percent annually. Similar competition is often available for natural gas.

Several years ago, Western began drawing on wind-driven energy, which is an option offered by many major vendors. Obviously, the electricity comes into our church on the same power lines, but our power now originates in wind generating fields of West Virginia. Since our congregation is committed to protecting the environment, we decided the small premium required to access wind-driven electrical power was a legitimate benevolence expense. Therefore, we have the basic charge for electricity in the building section of the budget. The premium for wind-driven energy is found in the benevolences. We also state in the Sunday bulletin that our electrical power is driven by the wind.

Of course, effective building management can reduce utility costs. Simple strategies like turning off lights, reducing the temperature settings on thermostats with timers, and having employees shut off their computers when they leave for the day can make a big difference.

INSURANCE

Careful management of insurance costs can save a congregation thousands of dollars annually. The key issues are the size of the deductible and the amount of liability coverage.

Many congregations pay extra for a low deductible. If the congregation files lots of small claims annually, the expense of this option is justified. However, if a congregation is not filing a lot of claims, it is probably smarter to "self-insure" by using a higher deductible.

For example, a congregation decided to raise its deductible from $500 to $5,000 per claim. The higher deductible reduced the annual premium from $10,000 to $7,500. During the course of the following year, the congregation filed four claims of $1,000 each. Under the old policy, the congregation would have paid a total of $2,000 in deductibles (4 times $500) for the four claims while the insurance company also paid $2,000 (4 times $500). Under the new policy, the congregation had to pay the entire $4,000 (4 times $1,000). But the lower premium meant that the congregation saved $500 overall. Under the new policy, the congregation paid a $7,500 premium and $4,000 in deductible expense for a total yearly insurance expense of $11,500. Under the old policy, it would have paid a $10,000 premium and $2,000 in deductible expense for a total of $12,000. Using this kind of analysis of the deductible options is important if a congregation wants to manage its insurance expense.

The amount of liability insurance a congregation carries is another important expense to analyze. In our litigious times, a church must have significant liability coverage. If a visitor has a bad accident on church property, the congregation may get sued. If a staff member is engaged in sexual misconduct, a congregation will most likely get sued. Therefore, significant coverage is important. Yet it is easy to overinsure for liability. To do so means needless expense. Insurance brokers familiar with the lives of congregations give good advice in making these decisions, taking into consideration factors such as whether or not the congregation operates a van or bus, both of which add liability exposure.

A group of our laypeople recently analyzed our insurance coverage. By fine-tuning our coverage, lowering our deductible, and eliminating "terrorism coverage" (this is a Washington, D.C. problem), we were able to reduce our annual insurance expense by approximately 30 percent. I questioned dropping the terrorism coverage, but our treasurer stopped me by asking, "Who is going to be around to file the claim after a terrorism attack?!?" Insurance coverage reviews don't need to happen annually since the conditions surrounding a congregation's insurance needs don't tend to change frequently. Nonetheless, policies should be reviewed every two or three years.

Finally, it's worth pointing out that there are relatively few companies that insure congregations. Most major insurance companies will not provide insurance to churches. As a result, the ability to pit one carrier against another in a competitive manner is limited. However, each congregation should try to obtain bids from several carriers if at all possible.

LEGAL MATTERS

My major concern when it comes to legal issues is the problem of using church members as the congregation's attorney. Lawyers have specialties just as physicians do. Would we want a cardiac surgeon giving us advice on our possible cancer? Not unless the cardiac surgeon was the only doctor within miles.

Too often, congregations rely on a church member who is an attorney for legal advice on a matter about which the attorney is not fully knowledgeable. The member may be a tax attorney but is giving advice on liability exposure for a staff member's sexual misconduct. The attorney may get it right. But he or she may get it wrong. If that happens, someone is going to ask, "Why didn't we get the proper advice?"

Yes, I know seeking outside counsel costs money. However, legal issues, if not dealt with properly, usually cost money too. Lots of money. So my advice is that congregations utilize outside legal help when dealing with any problem outside the expertise of the attorneys in the congregation. Might someone's nose get bent out of shape if this happens? Perhaps. But being an effective manager sometimes means explaining the obvious to those for whom it isn't obvious. Seeking outside opinions isn't a slight. It is common sense.

Managing Technology

The church's primary role in the world is to communicate the gospel through word and deed. In the 16th century, Martin Luther was able to get Scripture into the hands of his generation via the new technology of the printing press. Our generation is utilizing a wealth of new technologies to spread the gospel. Church secretaries rejoice that copiers, scanners, and computers have allowed them to abandon the challenging mimeo machines used to produce church bulletins in years past. More importantly, churches can now get the word out to their members and the world using e-mail, podcasts, blogs, Facebook, and websites. These tools have opened possibilities for spreading and teaching the gospel that previously couldn't have been imagined.

Ten years ago, most visitors found Western Church through word of mouth or an ad in *The Washington Post*. Today, they often find us by doing a Web search for Presbyterian congregations in Washington, D.C. After skimming through our website, first time visitors come to Western with a much better sense of whether it will be a church they will enjoy, one whose theology and mission will resonate with their own.

However, this book is not about all the things we can do in ministry with new information technologies. Here, we'll limit ourselves to the key management issues related to those technologies, including:

1. Acquiring and maintaining technology equipment such as computers, printers, modems, and cable/DSL connections.
2. Keeping the website updated, posting podcasts, and sending e-mail blasts to the congregation.
3. Date backups, remote access, and tech support.

In the twenty-first century, these management tasks are as important as keeping the lights on and the hot water hot.

ACQUIRING AND MAINTAINING EQUIPMENT

I make no claim to be an expert on computers and related technologies. But I do have some insight into managing the enormous changes in information technology that have changed the life of many congregations. Back in 1984, a Western member bought us a computer for about $2,500. It had 20 megabytes of space on the hard disk. We wondered how anyone would ever be able to use so much space. Our last computer was purchased for $450 and has a hard disk with 500 gigabytes! In the beginning of the Internet era, we used slow, cumbersome, dial-up modems. Today, we operate with a DSL connection. Twenty years ago, we didn't even know what a local area network (LAN) was, let alone utilize one. Today, our staff can work remotely from home, communicate with one another, and access both shared files and the Internet using a LAN. Our printer/copier communicates with the LAN via a wireless connection, saving the cost of cabling. Over the years, we've discarded more computers and software programs that I can count. Like so many of us, I have had to learn a great deal to stay current with recent technological advances.

Among the biggest challenges in managing technology is staying on top of the ever-changing options. The biggest errors in technology management involve buying in to new hardware or software too early or too late. Buy in too early, and you'll be dealing with bugs that haven't been worked out. Buy in too late, and you'll end up wasting a lot of time with programs and equipment that are slower than newer technologies allow.

Make no mistake about it: The technology manager does *not* have to be the pastor. I do it because I enjoy it. In most congregations, the technology manager is the secretary or administrative assistant, who often works with a knowledgeable layperson. The problem with having a volunteer layperson totally in charge of the technology is that keeping the church up-to-date technologically is not that person's job. When the LAN goes down or a computer crashes, it needs to be dealt with in a matter of minutes, not hours or days. A volunteer may be available by phone to give advice. However, there needs to be someone on the staff responsible for managing technology.

The ideal situation is to have a staff person who manages the technology with support from a layperson or small committee. To stay current, one needs to do a lot of reading, have firsthand experience with new products, and talk regularly with others who are managing technology. In my case, the executive director of our feeding program for the homeless loves technology. He and I help each other make decisions.

We all want the latest technological bells and whistles at our fingertips. However, the bells and whistles have a price tag. I was amazed at how quickly people changed from the older style, bulky monitors to flat-screen monitors. Yes, flat monitors are very cool looking, free up space on a desk, and add some things to the viewing experience. However, did everybody need to rush out and replace their old monitors with brand-new flat-screens? Not really. When many organizations were changing over to flat-screens, they were priced in the $500-$900 range. Today, it is easy to find a functional flat-screen for under $200. Organizations that waited a couple of years to upgrade their monitors saved thousands of dollars.

Cost-benefit analysis is crucial when it comes to technology. For example, does every staff member need a printer at her or his desk or will a network printer suffice? In our building, the associate pastor must walk down a long hallway and then down a set of stairs to get to the network printer. For this reason, a printer in the associate pastor's office is necessary. But we have found that one high-efficiency network color printer is sufficient for the entire staff. Each staff member can print black and white documents at his or her desk—but everyone walks to get the documents requiring color. Since color ink cartridges are very expensive, this is an efficient system.

When and what to buy, therefore, are at the heart of good technology management. Distinguishing between what is needed and what is possible is crucial. However, we must remember that technology can greatly increase our productivity. So cost has to be evaluated against time gained.

STAYING UP-TO-DATE

Many organizations spend an enormous amount to create a new website, then spend almost nothing to maintain it. This makes no sense. The power of a website is its ability to present up-to-date information to those who visit. Putting all the effort and money into design and almost nothing into maintenance is self-defeating.

As I look for information about congregations, I see this over and over again. Since what is popular in website design changes with time, it is fairly easy to figure out when a site was created. For example, prior to 2008, many designers used a the-more-information-on-the-home-page-the-better approach. More recently, designers have moved to a sleek, symbol-driven home page with links to access more information. But it's also easy to figure out the state of a congregation's website by looking at time-sensitive material. When I looked for a sermon by a friend of mine, the most recently posted sermon on the church site was eight months old. Clearly no one was updating the website on a regular basis.

Would we put an outdated calendar in the church newsletter or bulletin? Of course not. Why is there an outdated calendar on the website? Would we leave the names of departed staff people in the bulletin? Of course not. Why are these names still on so many websites? Would we leave sermon transcripts from six months ago in the narthex? Of course not. Why aren't these sermons in an archives file on the website?

I suppose any website is better than no website (although I'm not sure). Even the weakest sites include the church address and phone number. But don't expect a website to be a useful tool in ministry unless someone is actively, aggressively managing its content. If a ministry is changing, the website needs to change with it.

It is possible to do some pretty impressive things with a website as a launching pad. Like many churches, we include each week's sermon on the site in text form. More recently, we decided to make our sermons available as podcasts. To do so is fairly simple, involving a sound editing program, storage space on a site like www. podhoster.com, and a free software program like Filezilla to upload the audio file to podhoster. Once it's uploaded, we place the sermon on our own, free space at iTunes called The Progressive Christian Voice. The entire process of editing and uploading takes about fifteen minutes each week to stay current. At first, there was no connection between our website and the podcasts. Now we have an icon on the homepage of the site, linking the visitor to our podcasts. The number of people taking advantage of this ministry goes as high as eight hundred weekly. In addition, I e-mail my sermons to about two hundred fifty people weekly, most of whom are not members of our church. So even though the attendance at Sunday morning worship numbers about two hundred, an additional three hundred to one thousand people hear or read each sermon via e-mail or podcast. All this proclamation of the gospel requires maintenance and constant updating. E-mails change. Out-of-date podcasts need to be removed from podhoster and iTunes.

Who manages the website in your congregation? Is it a committee? If yes, this may explain why it isn't updated promptly. Committees are fabulous for many tasks in ministry, but they are not well suited for tedious, time sensitive work such as updating a website or maintaining accurate e-mail lists. An individual needs to be in charge of this responsibility.

Although the webmaster should report to the staff person responsible for managing technology, the webmaster does not need to be a staff person. Geeks are present in our pews! Put them to work. The work can be done by a volunteer as long as he or she is willing to devote weekly time to updates. Somebody on the staff still needs to be heavily involved, supplying the webmaster with current information.

Keeping websites updated and current is a classic management task. It requires a small strategic plan with simple goals. Once in place, the manager makes sure the people, financial, and hardware inputs are in place and used efficiently.

DATA BACKUPS, REMOTE ACCESS, AND TECHNICAL SUPPORT

One of the greatest assets of having a server as part of your church office's LAN is the backup capacity it creates. Every computer in a church can be linked to the server, which enables all files from the networked computers to be stored there. All the system needs is a backup timed to do its work during the night.

It is hard to overestimate the importance of backing up data. For example, most congregations do their financial work using software such as Quickbooks. In like manner, many congregations use software to track member information and giving. It is labor intensive to input all that data. Once lost, it may be impossible to replicate it. We don't want to lose the data. Back it up.

If there are files a staff member doesn't want stored on a public server (even though they can be made secure with a password), these can be stored on the C disk of that individual's desktop. I don't recommend this because we all forget to back up files. The easier route is to store everything on the public server and use passwords for sensitive files.

A church can also set up its system to allow staff members remote access to e-mail and data stored on the server. For about $700, a church can purchase software such as Microsoft Exchange that will allow staff members to access church related e-mail from home as easily as if they were sitting in the office. It gives the staff access not only to inbox e-mail they haven't read but also their saved, sent, and other mail folders.

Remote access to files through a virtual private network (VPN) likewise makes staff more efficient. I no longer have to drive to church if I want to get important files from my computer there. I can access all my computer-based files through the VPN. This major aid to ministry costs nothing to set up. The ability to set up a VPN is included as a basic component in all major computer operating systems.

No matter how a congregation's technology is managed, it is important to have professional tech support that can answer questions and, when necessary, do work. There are times when "stuff happens." At those times, churches need people who know what they're talking about and who, when necessary, can promptly pay a visit to the church to fix the problem. If the congregation has a server (these are now very affordable), the tech support company can access the system remotely, eliminating both the delays involved in driving to the site and the added cost of on-site visits. The secretary or administrative assistant should, at a minimum, be able to reboot both the cable/DSL modem and the server. Many problems can be solved with nothing more than a reboot of the system.

The Role of Trustees
or the Facilities Committee

Where possible, a congregation should have a group of laypeople that works with the staff's facilities management team. I say "where possible" because, in smaller churches, it is simply impossible to have a committee for every responsibility. If a small church attempts to replicate the governing model of a large church, it will be inefficient and will burn out members who must serve on multiple committees.

A facilities committee is most helpful when it devotes its energy to long-term issues rather than micromanaging the facilities staff. Because the staff is always addressing short-term problems, it is easy for them to pay insufficient attention to the bigger issues. Planning for long-term maintenance, setting up a capital reserve fund, and educating the congregation on the needs of the building are appropriate activities for a building committee or board of trustees. If a committee member feels the building isn't being cleaned adequately, it's appropriate for him or her to tell the head of staff. But allowing every member to instruct the janitor about how he or she should clean is inappropriate, regardless of the congregation's size.

Therefore, the key for a facilities committee or board is to develop the fine balance between management and micromanagement. The head of staff can be very helpful in enabling the committee or board to find that balance and in pointing out when the line is being crossed. Such advice may not always be well received by the committee, but it will be very much appreciated by the staff. Since pastors, janitors, and secretaries come and go, it is important for a congregation to build a corporate memory regarding the facilities. A facilities committee can play this role.

Some additional things a facilities committee can do:

- Create a long-term facilities management strategy including a schedule of anticipated replacement expenditures.
- Do the time-consuming work of evaluating insurance and utility options.
- Maintain detailed records regarding the service and installation of all the major facilities systems. These documents should be located in the building (along with any warranty verifications) so that staff and contractors can access them when questions arise. The congregation's financial person will also need access to the warranties.
- Manage blueprints for the church building, making sure duplicate copies of all prints are kept somewhere other than the church. In Western's old building, we were blessed to have the drawings from 1930. They were a godsend.

Finally, given the critical role that computers and related communication technology can play in the spreading of the gospel, it can be helpful if one or more individuals on the facilities committee are "tech-savvy." Since new technology can be expensive, it is helpful to have a small strategic plan regarding the goals of a congregation's use of technology, what technology the congregation needs to purchase, as well as a phased plan for funding and making the purchases. A facilities committee can play a valuable role in the formation of such a plan.

It's All Connected

We have identified three primary inputs for ministry: facilities, personnel, and finances. When it comes to management, facilities cannot be separated from the other two essential inputs. Good management of facilities requires the effective use of both people and financial resources. Yet if facilities are not managed properly, they can potentially overwhelm both the personnel and finances of a congregation. Poorly maintained facilities can require so much money and staff time that there is little time to engage in other aspects of ministry.

A systems approach to facilities (with a number of subsystems such as electrical, technology, and plumbing) enables managers to keep the facilities' input properly scaled to the other key inputs of ministry. Analyzing a system's individual parts within their larger context, we can see how they come together into a whole. Seeing the whole, we can more easily do solid planning and create adequate funding. When a congregation understands its facilities systems, hires the right personnel to maintain them, finds ways to adequately fund the short- and long-term needs of the facilities, covers its legal bases, and clarifies the role of the trustees or building committee, its facilities can become, not a barrier to ministry, but an effective part of our mission in spreading the gospel.

Manager's Checklist

- Assemble the key personnel inputs for facilities work, including people for cleaning, maintenance, various trades, and tech support. How much of the work can be done by hired staff? How much is best outsourced? What can be done by volunteers? How can existing staff's strengths be maximized?

- Analyze the current and future needs for the facilities, including the computer and communications technology, and create a schedule for anticipated repairs and replacement.
- Work with congregational leaders to begin setting aside money to fund long-term capital repairs and replacement.
- Create a short list of experts to be consulted for legal and insurance issues.
- When meeting with laypeople assigned oversight responsibilities for the facilities, clarify roles and responsibilities regarding management and staff.
- Identify and utilize church members with computer-related skills in the management of technology.

chapter 4

Managing
Church Finances

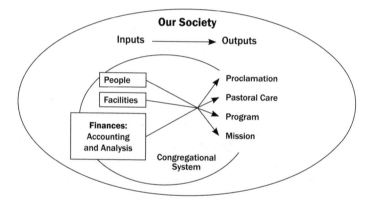

FIGURE 4.1 Financial Inputs

ystemically, the three inputs for ministry are interrelated. The personnel and facilities of a congregation cannot be separated from its finances. Without money, a congregation will not be able to secure and maintain the necessary facilities for ministry. Without money, a congregation will be limited to using volunteers rather than adding paid staff where necessary. Effective handling of finances helps a congregation make the most out of what it has been given by God and its members so that it can accomplish its goals in ministry.

My understanding of ministry—and particularly its financial aspects—has been shaped by Jesus' parable of the pounds (Luke 19:11–27). In the parable, a nobleman gives money to three different servants, telling each to "do business" with the funds until he returns. Two invest the money wisely, double it, and earn the rich man's praise. But the third, fearing he might lose the money he was given, buries it in the ground—and earns the nobleman's scorn.

I call this the "entrepreneurial parable." Jesus commends to his listeners the two investors who increase their holdings, not the one who is fearfully risk-averse. As congregations manage their finances, can they embrace the theology of this parable? Can they resist the temptation to play it safe and take reasonable risks with what they've been given to accomplish God's mission in the world?

To manage its financial holdings in ways that lead to their growth, a congregational strategic plan should have some goal or objectives specifically addressing the manner in which money will be handled. For example, one goal might be to have a transparent, well-monitored financial system. That goal might include specific objectives relating to the way money is handled, how budgets and financial decisions are made and communicated to the congregation, and clear linkages between money received and the ministry enabled by those funds. Considering financial issues in the context of a congregation's strategic plan will allow for a healthy, needed conversation about the values underlying the handling of money and the congregation's priorities in ministry.

Every congregation must consider whether it wants to protect its financial position at all costs or maximize it by taking some risks. Strategies relating to endowments or special fundraising drives (for buildings, program, or mission) often evoke these questions. Does a congregation use only a percentage of the annual earnings from an endowment or does it take what it needs to achieve the strategic goals it has set and not worry about the size of the endowment? Does a congregation dedicate all the money raised in a special fundraising drive to the planned addition to its church building or does it take a risk that the campaign will raise enough money to include some additional funds for benevolent giving?

Placing finances in the strategic plan will also create specific strategies for safeguarding the way a congregation's money is handled, invested, and set aside for anticipated future needs. The strategies require management by individuals who are dedicated to details. Congregations that don't attend to management details either waste money or have it stolen. When this happens, opportunities to glorify God are missed. With sound financial practices in place and wise management of these practices, the congregation will exhibit faithful stewardship of its financial life. Congregations with good financial management are also less likely to be the victim of fraud or theft. Incredibly, such crimes against the church happen almost daily in the United States.

When I first was called to Western Presbyterian Church in 1983, the finances were being run much like those of a mom-and-pop store. With revenue and expense of about $80,000 each, we basically had just two budget categories—revenue and expense. There was very little detail describing the sources of revenue and expense. My experience with other congregations has taught me that this kind of simplistic approach is all too common in many churches. Too often, congregations focus almost entirely on the financial bottom line ("Are we in the positive or negative?") and not on the details of how the bottom line is generated. My goal in this chapter is to explain why, when it comes to accounting, the devil is *not* in the details; instead, faithful stewardship is in the details. To that end, we'll consider the following points:

- Congregational managers don't need to be accountants. However, they need a basic understanding of how accounting works and what kinds of financial statements can be produced.
- Financial data can be used in a variety of ways. The more methods of interpretation and analysis a manager knows and uses, the more effective the management of finances will be.
- A well-functioning finance committee can provide financial oversight and, very importantly, create money-handling practices that reduce the likelihood of fraud or theft.

In the pages ahead, we'll take a brief look at the basic principles of a good financial management system. After a basic introduction to accounts and financial reports, we'll consider various accounting methods, look at ways of using and interpreting financial data, examine systemic issues related to the finance committee and approaches to dealing with money, and conclude with some thoughts on fundraising.

I can already feel the anxiety level rising for some readers. I know that many clergy and laypeople grow uncomfortable when the topic turns to bookkeeping and accounting. But fear not—it is actually a fun journey! In fact, by the time you reach the end of this chapter, you should be able to complete successfully the simple accounting exercises you'll find in appendix C.

An Introduction to Accounts and Financial Reports

We begin with the distinction between bookkeeping and accounting. The finance department of any corporation includes individuals engaged in both activities. Congregations need both activities as well.

Bookkeepers record financial events. For example, a church offering is received on Sunday morning. A financial event has happened; money has been received. After the money is counted, it is recorded by a bookkeeper. The event is memorialized in the church's financial records by a bookkeeping journal entry.

Accounting takes the activity of bookkeeping to a more sophisticated level where financial statements are generated for analysis and fiscal problems are solved. First and foremost, an accounting system defines a methodology for assigning revenues and expenses to accounts. In the case of the Sunday offering, the accounting system tells the bookkeeper which account should be used for the offering. In an extremely simple accounting system, the bookkeeper would simply record the entire offering under an account named "Offering Income." In a more informed system, the counters would separate the offering into different types of income (such as pledges, open plate, and gifts from regular attendees). With a journal entry, the bookkeeper then posts the income from each category into the appropriate account. This allows a congregation to understand the source of its revenue in more detail.

With accurate bookkeeping and well-defined accounts, accountants can generate two basic financial reports—an income statement and a balance sheet—as well as an up-to-date cash-flow document. These three snapshots of a congregation's financial life, when used properly, give pastors, governing bodies, and congregations a comprehensive understanding of a congregation's financial situation at a specific moment in time.

- An *income statement* displays the revenue and expense for a congregation for a given period of time (month, quarter, or year). After totaling all the revenue and expense, the expense is subtracted from the revenue to produce the famous "bottom line"—the budget surplus or deficit.
- A *balance sheet* displays the assets and liabilities of a congregation at a particular point of time. When the liabilities are subtracted from the assets, the resulting number reveals the net financial worth of a congregation (in terms of physical, tangible assets that can be reflected in dollars in a financial statement).
- The *cash flow report* provides a snapshot of the congregation's current cash position—how much cash it has on hand. In the business world, a cash flow document is produced starting with net profits for the period under consideration. For a congregation, the cash flow report is built from the *cash journal*. As an accounting professor once told me, the cash journal functions the way a checkbook used to function in an individual's finances: It keeps track of where money goes and how much is left on hand.

While an income statement shows revenue and expenses charged against accounts for a given period, it does not show the overall cash position of a congregation. Obviously, understanding a congregation's cash position with a well kept cash journal is extremely important (at least it is to me, since I like my salary to be paid regardless of any cash-flow problems). The journal reveals how cash has been used during a period as well as how much cash is on hand.

Differences in the timing of expenses and revenue can cause wide variations in a congregation's cash position over the course of a year. For example, most congregations experience a cash shortage in the summer, since many members pay their pledges toward the end of the year. The cash flow journal helps a congregation understand and manage its cash position so it has enough cash available throughout the year to meet ongoing responsibilities.

In this chapter, we will first learn about these three basic financial tools—the income statement, balance sheet, and cash journal. As we grasp the information needed to use these tools, we will also grasp the basics of financial accounting. All three of these tools are generated by a basic bookkeeping and accounting system that involves journal entries that are posted to various accounts. Even though these journal entries are usually entered into a computerized accounting program (rather than processed by hand) I believe it's important to understand the basic system so we can see how information to be used in financial reports is generated. Therefore, we begin this section by developing an understanding of journal entries and T-accounts. Readers who are not interested in going into this type of depth regarding accounting can skip to the section entitled "Income Statements" and resume reading there.

T-ACCOUNTS AND JOURNAL ENTRIES

The heart of any accounting system is in the accounts! And, unlike trying to understand human behavior, understanding accounts is relatively simple. *Accounts are used to record transactions that either increase or decrease assets, liabilities, expense, and revenue.* We'll look at how these four accounts are related to one another later in the chapter.

In the past, all accounts were traditionally maintained by hand using journal entries and T-accounts (which are so named because of their physical format in older style manual bookkeeping). While none of us will probably ever see a T-account (computerized

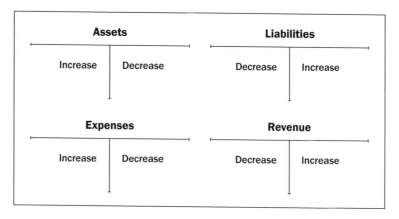

FIGURE 4.2 T Accounts

accounting programs have replaced them), we need to understand the T-account to understand accounting. On either side of the vertical line in the T, we record increases and decreases in accounts (see Figure 4.2). The famous terms *debit* and *credit* are related to the T-account. *Debit* means "record on the left side" and *credit* "record on the right side." Increases in assets and expenses as well as decreases in liabilities and revenues are *debited*. Decreases in assets and expenses as well as increases in liabilities and revenues are *credited*. (An easy way to remember this is your debit cash card. Do you have more or less cash when you use it? Debits in a revenue account *reduce* the available revenue.

There is a basic rule for T accounts: Whatever is taken away from one T-account (debited or credited) must be added (credited or debited) to another T-account. The principle is not unlike the old axiom that says "What God giveth, God taketh away." When money is spent (given away) from one account, it has to be reflected in (taken from) another account. (There is definitely a sermon in this accounting practice.) For example, one cannot increase (debit) assets without increasing (credit) revenues or liabilities. Figure 4.3 (on page 108) shows how the credit/debit system works with a T-account. (At times, accounts will have dual functions. For example, cash is an asset. However, as an asset, it also serves to record incoming cash revenues or outgoing cash for expenses.)

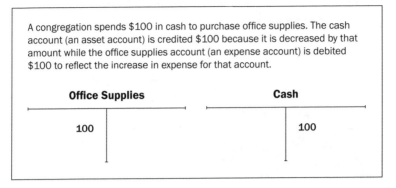

A congregation spends $100 in cash to purchase office supplies. The cash account (an asset account) is credited $100 because it is decreased by that amount while the office supplies account (an expense account) is debited $100 to reflect the increase in expense for that account.

Office Supplies

100

Cash

100

FIGURE 4.3 Credit/Debit System

Prior to being entered in T-accounts, all financial transactions are recorded using journal entries. Until recently, journal entries were made by hand in an actual journal, similar to the entry below in Figure 4.4. In computerized programs, the journal entry is usually made on a page that resembles a checkbook. Any journal entry charging an expense to one account must have a corresponding entry in another account to explain the source of the payment. Any revenue received to an account such as cash must have a corresponding entry reflecting the expense account in which the revenue was assigned. (The distinction between revenue and income is important. Revenue is any money received; income is arrived at by subtracting expense from revenue.)

For example, if a congregation spends $50 for new altar candles, the $50 is debited under an expense account named "Wor-

	Debit	Credit
Worship Supplies	50	
Cash		50

FIGURE 4.4 Journal Entries

ship Supplies." If cash was used for the purchase, a revenue account named "Cash" is then credited with a corresponding entry of $50: Or, consider a congregation that receives a bequest gift of $20,000, as seen below in Figure 4.5. Ultimately, it will receive the gift in the form of cash (a check). To help the congregation understand the multiple sources of its cash (which is crucial for financial forecasting), the money is received in a revenue account named "Bequests" that will display as a revenue account on the Income Statement. It is then reflected in another revenue account "Cash" that will display as an asset on the balance sheet with a corresponding entry.

	Debit	Credit
Cash	20,000	
Bequests		20,000

FIGURE 4.5 Journal Entries

In Figure 4.6 below, we see how a bookkeeper might record the Sunday morning offering for a congregation. He or she records the income as cash in the cash account while, for purposes of identification, recording it in the pledge, nonmember, and open-plate

The congregation has received $5,000 in the morning offering. The counters indicate that $3,000 was from pledges, $1,200 was from regular nonmember givers, and $800 was from visitors. The journal entry will be as follows:

	Debit	Credit
Cash	5,000	
Pledge Revenue		3,000
Nonmember Revenue		1,200
Open Plate Revenue		800

FIGURE 4.6 Journal Entries

revenue accounts. (While cash is an asset account, it also serves as another purpose regarding transactions that relate to the income statement. It reflects cash coming in as revenue and going out for expenses.) These entries result in the cash account being increased by the $5,000 received while the nature of the receipt (pledge, non-member, and open plate) is identified for accounting purposes including tax records, analysis, and future budget-preparation.

As the pastor of a congregation, the key is to make sure the church employs a bookkeeper who makes accurate journal entries. These entries are simple to make, but they are a nightmare to correct if made incorrectly. Furthermore, a congregation wants to make sure its accountant has designed a system of accounts that gives the bookkeeper an adequate range of accounts to which expense and revenue can be posted in the journal. The bookkeeper may need to consult the accountant occasionally regarding which account should be debited or credited for a particular revenue or expense event.

The most common conversation I have with my treasurer relates to the assignment of expense and revenue. For example, I recently purchased a new multimedia projector to use for Power-Point presentations. The projector will be used mostly for Christian education so I suggested charging the CE account. The treasurer rightly felt the expense should be charged to the equipment purchase account because the projector will be used in ways other than Christian education. A second issue in this transaction is the capitalization of the expense. The disbursement produces an asset (the projector). It needs to be recorded as an asset so it will show up on the balance sheet as such. So, again, we see how a single purchase results in more than one type of entry. In this case, it has to be recorded as an expense and the books have to show that cash was used to pay for it. It also needs to be recorded as an asset.

A church might have similar issues regarding how revenues are allocated. For example, I've asked our treasurer to create a line item to receive special gifts and bequests. This allows our congregation's financial managers, including me, to identify and track that particular revenue stream. The key for projecting revenues from year to year is to track revenues in a way that distinguishes between those revenues that will be recurring and those that will not.

Now let's take some time to examine each of the three key financial statements in a bit more detail.

BALANCE SHEET ACCOUNTS

In the case of a congregation, the list of asset accounts typically will include cash on hand, savings, land, building, property, and perhaps an endowment or memorial funds. Liabilities might include a mortgage, other forms of debt, as well as any type of unmet financial commitment for which the congregation is legally liable. (For example, perhaps the congregation owes a lay employee a pension or a tax liability for IRS withholding.)

To create a balance sheet, each individual account is totaled. Each account begins with a balance to which all increases are added and decreases subtracted, resulting in a new balance. The new balances of the various accounts are displayed in the appropriate asset and liability sections of the balance sheet. The difference between the total assets and liability accounts produces the net worth of the congregation. An example of a balance sheet can be found in appendix A.

Assets of a congregation tend to have a fixed nature. Buildings, memorial funds, cash, and other typical assets may change in value but they usually continue to exist (unless the entire asset category is sold or otherwise disposed of). Since the major liability for most congregations is a mortgage, hopefully the liabilities are decreasing over time. Few congregations have no liabilities.

How things are valued is a key issue in recording transactions in asset and liability accounts. Accountants can choose between book value and current value. For example, is the value of a congregation's van the current market value of that vehicle (what the vehicle could be sold for) or the book value (the cost of the vehicle at purchase less depreciation)? When book value is used, depreciation is subtracted periodically from the asset's original value to create a new (book) value.

The issues of book versus current value and the role of depreciation are important because the net worth of the congregation can dramatically increase or decrease depending on the choice made. For example, the congregation I serve has seen its property double in value over the past nine years. Therefore, the current value would seem to be more relevant than the depreciated book value (only the building, not the land, can be depreciated) for understanding the worth of this key asset. Using current value will also create a significantly higher net worth (assuming property values have increased).

However, many accountants dislike using market value as a measure of worth because we open a Pandora's box of possibilities. (Accountants hate multiple possibilities!) For example, we include the value of our building as a depreciating asset on our balance sheet. Yet the value of the building itself is fundamentally irrelevant to the overall value of our property, since any developer purchasing the property would tear the building down. The actual value of our property is not the combined value of the building and property but rather the value of the property. Therefore, should we list only the current market value of the property or the book value of the property and building?

Generally accepted accounting principles (GAAP) call for book value to be used. GAAP uses this conservative method because it ensures that entities don't overvalue their assets based on an assumed current value. To see the problems that can occur when current values are used, we need only look at the economic crisis of 2008–2009. Certainly, the crisis has multiple causes, but one major cause was financial institutions putting too much faith in current values of bundled real estate securities they held. When real estate markets, infamous for their "bubbles," began to collapse, the current value of the bundled securities acting as collateral for loans decreased. The relationship between assets and liabilities became skewed—and the crisis was on.

Using book value avoids the problems inherent in efforts to "discern" a current market value each year. However, book value is not without its own problems. Computers provide a classic example of why book value can be very misleading. If a congregation purchases a computer for $1,000, one year later it is probably worth $100. Unless one creates a depreciation schedule that ac-knowledges the rapid loss of value for a computer (in this exam-ple, 90 percent in one year), recording the purchase value in the assets will lead to an inflated asset balance.

Another balance sheet issue involves how pledges are treated. I prefer to see pledges treated the way a business treats accounts receivable (an asset account). Accounts receivable are money con-tractually owed to a business. Similarly, a pledge represents a con-tract in which a church member promises to give a certain amount to the church. The pledge is, in effect, money contractually (or at least morally) owed to the congregation by a member. The giving of congregations is relatively predictable. When members pledge, we know approximately how much of that money will actually be paid. In the congregation I serve, it is roughly 99 percent. In other congregations, I have heard of the pay-up being 90 to 99 percent. These pay-up rates are as high or higher than pay-ups of many ac-counts receivable in a business. Therefore, I think pledged income (discounted by the historic pay-up rate) should be treated as an as-set. Unfortunately, some congregations don't list pledged income as an asset. The pledges exist in the mind of the treasurer or on some informal bookkeeping system but not in the financial statements of the congregation. This is not a transparent approach to accounting.

THE INTERPLAY OF REVENUE, EXPENSE, ASSET, AND LIABILITY ACCOUNTS

For a congregation, the bookkeeping for revenue and expense as well as asset and liability accounts is somewhat less complicated than the issues involved in balance sheet decisions. It isn't essential for every manager to understand the finer details of all aspects of accounting, but it is essential for managers to understand, func-tionally if not perfectly, the interplay between revenue, expense, asset, and liability accounts. Unless we understand this, we cannot understand the way money is booked and dispersed by the congre-gation's financial system.

Revenue and expense accounts are very straightforward re-cordings of revenue received and expense paid—"cash in, cash out." There are two primary issues with these accounts: *when* the expense or revenue is assigned and *to what account* a particular revenue or expense is assigned. In general, revenue will increase an asset account such as cash, bequests, or special gifts. Cash received in the Sunday morning offering, for example, will increase the asset account "Cash." Expenses will decrease an asset, usually cash, because money flows out while increasing the expense accounts to which the cost is assigned.

To show the interplay between revenue, expense, asset, and liability accounts, consider a congregation that pays its $1,000 annual premium for insurance on June 30. Since the payment is made mid-year, only six months of the expense can be assigned to the budget of the current calendar year. What does the bookkeeper do with the remaining six months of paid-up insurance so it will show up correctly in the following year's books? He or she assigns the expense for the remaining six months to an asset account called "Prepaid Insurance." This allows it to be carried into the new financial year on the balance sheet. In the following year, as the insurance is used, the "Prepaid Insurance" account will be reduced until it is zero on June 30. The insurance is considered an asset because it is a service for which the congregation has paid that will be used over a period of time. As the policy is used, it decreases in value until it is no longer an asset.

If the insurance still feels like just an expense, not an asset, think about it this way: If the policy were canceled, the congregation would get a cash refund from the insurance company for the unused portion. Therefore, the policy is an asset that can be transformed into cash. But in the new year, if it is not canceled, the asset is drained of its value as it is assigned to that year's insurance expense line item.

So when and where expenses are assigned is important. It is also important to fine tune how one accounts for cash. For most congregations, the primary sources of cash are payments on pledges due, open plate offerings, special gifts, and endowment funds. These traditional sources of congregational revenue generate the cash needed to pay expenses. For example, the journal entry in Figure 4.7 would be made to show the payment of $1,000 in pledges. Pledges made but not received are credited to Pledges Due, an as-

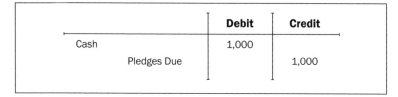

	Debit	Credit
Cash	1,000	
Pledges Due		1,000

FIGURE 4.7 Journal Entries

set account. (Remember the earlier comparison of pledges to a business having an Accounts Receivable asset account for revenue committed but not yet received.)

As revenue comes in, the Pledges Due asset account would be reduced (credited) by $1,000 and the Cash asset account would be increased (debited) by $1,000. This transaction records the Cash (asset) account rising and the Pledges Due (asset) account decreasing. If a congregation has $100,000 in pledges and everyone meets his or her commitment, by the end of the year the Cash account would have increased (been debited) by $100,000 and the Pledges Due account would have decreased (been credited) from $100,000 to $0. Note that the transaction is a wash for assets. The Cash increases by the exact same amount the Pledges Due decreases.

Of course, another way to generate revenue is to borrow cash. A loan creates a liability (a requirement to pay back the loan). Let's say that St. John's Church borrows $100,000 for a building renovation project. Figure 4.8 shows how one set of journal entries will show an increase in the asset Cash (debit) account and

	Debit	Credit
Cash	100,000	
Loan Amount		100,000
Renovations	100,000	
Cash		100,000

FIGURE 4.8 Journal Entries

an increase in the liabilities Loan (credit) account. Another set of entries will show an expense debit of the $100,000 for the building renovations with a corresponding credit entry reducing the Cash account. The net impact of loan on the balance sheet will be to increase both liabilities and assets by $100,000. The impact on the income statement will be to increase both revenues and expenses by $100,000.

Concurrently, the person or institution making the loan is creating a journal entry that shows a decrease of Cash (credit) and an increase in the asset (debit) account Loans Receivable. Again, there is zero impact on their balance sheet.

I don't believe every pastor needs to know all the bookkeeping details about how each account is being managed. However, I believe we should know the significant accounting issues affecting the overall cash positions of the congregations we serve. My accounting professor used to say, "If your accounting and finance people sense that you don't understand this material, they will own you!" We don't need to know all the details, but we do need to know enough to ask the right questions and not look at financial documents like deer staring at headlights. Indeed, asking the finance people whether an expense was incurred totally in the calendar year or partially prepaid for next year will instantly build your credibility!

The best people to teach us what we need to know are usually in our congregations, particularly since every set of books has its own unique stamp. Ask these people for help. They will gladly provide it.

THE INCOME STATEMENT

Bookkeeping done with journal entries and T-accounts allows a congregation to generate an income statement. In an income statement, all the accounts are reconciled as of a particular moment in time, producing a positive or negative number for the year to date. This allows managers to track revenue and expenses as a year unfolds. Remember that *reconciled* simply means taking the opening balance for an account, adding all the increases to that account, and subtracting the decreases. This creates a new balance that is shown on the appropriate line item in the income statement, and serves as the beginning balance for the next financial period. An example of an income statement can be found in appendix B.

The income statement begins with a revenue section that lists the various sources of revenue. All these accounts are added together to produce a figure for total revenue. Next there is an expense section that lists the various accounting allocations of expenses, which are added to create a total for expense. The famous "bottom line" simply subtracts expense from revenue to produce a positive or negative figure for the time period in question. Figure 4.9 below shows a very simple income statement that compares income and expenses from a particular month to the totals from the same month of the previous year.

If a church does not understand its sources of revenue, a sudden drop in overall revenue will be perplexing. However, if reve-

Income Statement for the Newkirk Congregation
May 2005

	2005	2004
Revenue		
Pledges	30,000	25,000
Open Plate	500	5,000
Building Use	4,000	3,000
Endowment Incomes	10,000	10,000
Special Gifts	1,500	2,000
Total Revenue	46,000	45,000
Expense		
Salaries & Benefits	21,000	19,000
Utilities	3,000	3,000
Program	2,000	1,500
Benevolence Giving	10,000	9,000
Administration	2,000	1,500
Mortgage	10,000	10,000
Total Expense	48,000	44,500
Surplus (Deficit)	(2,000)	500

FIGURE 4.9 Income Statement

nue is tracked carefully using an income statement, a congregation can better understand and manage its finances. For example, if the source of the overall drop in revenue is identified as a drop in giving by nonmembers (usually money placed in the offering plate by visitors), church leaders may conclude that the real problem is not financial but a drop in the number of visitors attending. If the revenue drop is traced to building use, church leaders can seek other groups and individuals who will generate new revenues using the church building—such as daycare centers, nonprofit groups, or weddings. Knowledge of where money comes from and where it goes gives church leaders the power to develop constructive responses to problems that manifest themselves in financial ways.

If revenue is holding steady but a deficit situation develops, it is necessary to examine carefully the expense side of the budget. Perhaps the congregation experienced an especially cold winter followed by a hot summer, causing utility expense to come in higher than budgeted. This might be viewed as an aberration (which would, therefore, require no budgetary changes) or it may be fiscally prudent to plan on higher utilities for the following year. Or consider another situation where the expense side of a congregation's budget is significantly below projections, helping to create an overall budget surplus. If analysis shows that the decreased spending was due to more efficient use of resources, it may be possible to plan for similar efficiencies in future budgets. However, if the lower spending was the result of a vacant staff position that needs to be filled, the congregation should not plan for the savings to continue.

Unless a congregation understands the causes of a budgetary surplus or deficit, it cannot plan future budgets in a responsible manner. By creating a comprehensive income statement that records revenue and expense, a congregation can engage in responsible fiscal analysis. The more accounts on the revenue and expense side that can be created, the better a congregation will know exactly what is driving its financial situation. For example, rather than a single expense line for salaries, a congregation may want to have different categories for pastoral, administrative, program and maintenance salaries. This would give church leaders a better idea of exactly what salaries are being spent on.

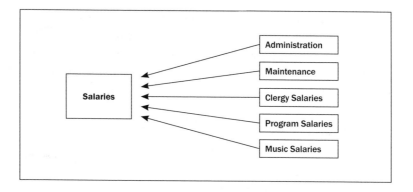

FIGURE 4.10 Creating Expense Detail

By breaking down expenses into more well-defined categories, we are able to understand and exert control over how much money is being spent for various church activities, including music, Christian education, and local mission. As always, knowledge is power.

THE CASH JOURNAL AND CASH REPORTS

In order to make sure sufficient funds are available to cover each month's expenses, the church treasurer needs to estimate those expenses. The treasurer also needs to estimate the amount of cash that will come in either through pledges, open plate giving, withdrawals from savings, or an endowment and from other sources.

Cash Journal 2004

Starting Balance, January 1				25,000	
Date	**Account**	**Debit**		**Credit**	**Balance**
1/1/2004	Insurance Premium			1,200	23,800
1/3/2004	Pastor's Salary			4,000	19,800
1/3/2004	Sexton Salary			2,000	17,800
1/5/2004	Sunday Offering	5,000			23,800

FIGURE 4.11 Cash Journal

Figure 4.11 (on page 119) shows how a cash journal is maintained. It is not unlike a checking account. A cash balance is at the top of every page, and credit and debit entries are made as well as the effect of that entry on the cash balance. By checking the cash journal, the treasurer can always know exactly how much cash is on hand.

Efficient cash management requires maintaining available cash that is sufficient but not excessive. If cash sitting in a checking account could be invested in some higher earning account, then it should be invested. Tracking and analyzing one's cash needs over the years will help the treasurer to perfect this task and increase investment returns.

Figure 4.12 on the previous page shows a very simple form of cash analysis. It is an annual summary of the cash journal on a monthly basis. Each month starts with a beginning balance, adds all cash revenue, and subtracts all cash expenses, resulting in an ending balance, which becomes the starting balance for the next month. Not much to it, but it is essential. You may notice that there was a negative bank balance in the month of May.

	1st of Month Bank Balance	Deposits & Other Credits	Checks Issued & Other Debits	Bank Balance
January	16,677.77	92,169.59	-98,275.28	10,572.08
February	10,572.08	135,435.39	-97,775.01	48,232.46
March	48,232.46	120,855.38	-121,802.54	47,285.30
April	47,285.30	49,793.84	-81,652.14	15,427.00
May	15,427.00	67,064.35	-104,748.02	-22,256.67
June	-22,256.67	162,253.46	-107,749.21	32,247.58
July	32,247.58	99,684.41	-103,490.34	28,441.65
August	28,441.65	104,226.25	-119,306.69	13,361.21
September	13,361.21	120,780.82	-96,175.09	37,966.94
October	37,966.94	82,538.05	-86,281.79	34,223.20
November	34,223.20	109,811.63	-121,086.18	22,948.65
December	22,948.65	152,399.45	-124,158.50	51,189.60

FIGURE 4.12 Cash Analysis

Why? Checks were written but "held." In the opening days of June, the congregation received revenue to cover the negative balance and avoided the checks bouncing.

ADVANTAGES OF STANDARD ACCOUNTING SYSTEMS

Why bother using this system of accounting and reporting finances in a church? There are several reasons.

First, it is a universal system that can be understood by anyone familiar with accounting. In an age when "financial transparency" has become crucial for financial credibility, the ability for anyone (including auditors, denominational officials, loan officers, or church members) to walk in and check a congregation's books, using a universally recognized system, is beyond important. It is essential.

Second, the accounting system allows those who manage church budgets to see the impact of funds coming in and funds going out. Too many congregations and clergy have a very loose understanding of how, when, and where money is spent. A tightly monitored system of debits and credits that generates accurate financial reports allows those in charge of the financial life of a congregation to know exactly where money is being spent and from what sources money is being drawn to meet the expenses.

Third, a standard debit and credit system with established accounts for revenue and expense makes it possible to total the accounts and generate a financial report at any point in time. Such financial reports, especially when designed with a column comparing current expenses and revenue year-to-date with those of the preceding year, provides financial managers with a quick, comprehensive picture of the financial status of the congregation.

Fourth, there is no better system to prevent fraud. On a regular basis, members of a congregation's finance committee need to conduct an internal audit to ensure that the precious giving of church members is being spent as promised. The auditors take vouchers submitted for cash dispersals, match them to the journal entries, and look at the software's printout of expenses for the account. It is a little tedious but can help assure that the financial aspects of a church's life are being handled with honesty and integrity.

Of course, it is impossible to create a financial system that will *guarantee* honesty. Pastors tell stories about money being skimmed off the collection plate by an usher, cash pocketed rather than recorded by the counters, financial staff misallocating funds, and lots of other horrors. We can't stop everything. But we can build a financial system that (1) increases the difficulty of perpetrating fraud, and (2) makes it easier to detect fraud when it occurs.

Some congregations generate financial reports on a monthly basis, others on a quarterly basis. With an accounting software program such as Intuit's *Quickbooks*, reports can be generated simply by hitting the appropriate command key. Such programs also provide the explanatory debit/credit background to each account, even showing the check number used to pay a particular voucher. Given the ease of producing reports, I don't know why any congregation would choose to review its finances any less than monthly.

Basic accounting is not rocket science. If I can learn to do it with my limited math skills, any seminary graduate can learn it. The only reason most clergy and lay leaders don't know the basics of accounting is because nobody bothered to teach us! Some of us learn as we go, others muddle through it all, and others run from financial issues. But when we understand accounting systems, we become wiser, more effective stewards of the limited resources of our congregations.

Using Financial Data More Effectively

The point of collecting and organizing the financial activity of a congregation is to ensures that its money is being used effectively toward its goals in ministry. There are a variety of ways to interpret financial data that can help congregations better understand how their money is being used and what they can expect in terms of future financial resources for ministry. These tools include activity-based costing, time series trend analysis, forecasting for budgeting and cash flow, understanding the opportunity cost of money, and auditing.

ACTIVITY-BASED COSTING

Activity-Based Costing (ABC) is widely used in the business world to gain better insight into the cost of each separate operation in a company. For example, a company that makes bicycles would seek to determine how much it costs to manufacture bike model A, market the bike, deliver it to the seller, and other relevant costs. They can then contrast this to the costs of manufacturing, marketing, and delivering bike model B.

The company might break down the manufacturing costs into ever-more-discrete units. By breaking down the costs from one lump sum to discrete units, managers have the opportunity to look for cost savings. It may turn out that the frame of model A can be made less expensively. Or perhaps they will discover their labor costs for model A are much higher than for model B, and they need to examine labor efficiencies.

This same approach to costs can be used in congregations. It has always bothered me that salaries and benefits are often lumped into one line item. Too often people will say, "We need to spend less money on salaries and more on mission." But aren't the staff being paid to do the mission? When we send money to support a school in Kenya, don't we call that money mission—even though a large portion of that money goes to teacher and administrative salaries?

ABC helps us to assign costs in a congregation so that we can see what activities our dollars are funding. Let us consider a congregation with salaries and benefits for two pastors ($80,000 and $60,000), a secretary ($45,000), a janitor ($30,000) and a part-time musician ($20,000). The main activities of the congregation are worship, pastoral care, Christian education, community mission, and music. The budget is displayed in Figure 4.13 (on page 124).

To understand what each aspect of this congregation's life costs, we begin by calculating a number for fixed costs. Fixed costs, in this example, include the costs that exist no matter what program is being done. Certainly building, grounds, and general administration

St. Mark's Budget
2005

	2005
Personnel	
Salaries & Benefits	235,000
Administration	35,000
Building & Grounds	125,000
Program	
Music	20,000
Christian Education	15,000
Mission/Community Outreach	100,000
Total	530,000

FIGURE 4.13 The Budget

costs fall into this category. I would argue that the secretary and janitor are also fixed costs. (There are congregations that have no installed pastor and relatively little program, yet still employ at least a part-time secretary and janitor.) Therefore, fixed costs for St. Mark's can be seen in Figure 4.14:

Building & Grounds	125,000
Administration	35,000
Secretary's Salary & Benefits	45,000
Janitor's Salary & Benefits	35,000
Pastor's General Administration	22,000
Total	262,000

FIGURE 4.14 Fixed Costs

To use ABC, the next task is to discern what percentage of the fixed costs should be assigned to worship, pastoral care, Christian education, community mission, and music. Of course, this can be a fairly arbitrary process. The various departments of a business can get into huge arguments when a particular department believes it is being assigned too large a percentage of the overhead costs. However, if we remain flexible in understanding the results of the process, these cost assignments are very helpful.

Given the size of the sanctuary (it costs a lot to heat and air-condition) as well as the attention to its maintenance and cleaning (janitor's time) and the amount of the secretary's time devoted to the Sunday bulletin, flowers, phone calls asking for information about worship, and other related activity, we will assign 50 percent of the overhead to worship. Christian education also utilizes a lot of physical space, which requires much of the janitor's attention. Therefore, 25 percent is assigned to Christian education, and pastoral care and mission/community outreach are each assigned 5 percent, since these activities require very little from the fixed costs items. Finally, 15 percent of the fixed costs are assigned to music, since the music program requires space as well as janitorial and secretarial support. The music program costs also includes 100 percent of the part-time musician's salary.

What about the time of the pastors? The head of staff estimates that she spends 30 percent of her time on worship, 30 percent on pastoral care, 20 percent on general administration (we will add this into the fixed costs since it covers all the programs), and 20 percent on community outreach activities. The associate pastor estimates that he spends 20 percent on worship, 20 percent on pastoral care, 50 percent on Christian education, and 10 percent on general administration (which is, again, added into fixed costs).

Using these cost assignments, Figure 4.15 (on page 126) reveals how the congregation is spending its money.

The results presented here paint a much different picture than what's seen in the traditional line-item budget. Pastoral care didn't even show up in the earlier budget approach. Using ABC, the congregation is now able to see that it is making a considerable investment in pastoral care.

ABC for St. Mark's Church			
Worship			
50% of Fixed Costs	128,000		
30% of Head of Staff	24,000		
20% of Associate Pastor	12,000		
		164,000	
Christian Education			
25% of Fixed Costs	64,2500		
50% of Associate Pastor	30,000		
Budget Line Item	15,000		
		109,250	
Music			
15% of Fixed Costs	38,550		
Part Time Musician	20,000		
Budget Line Item	20,000		
		78,550	
Pastoral Care			
10% of Fixed Costs	12,850		
30% of Head of Staff	24,000		
20% of Associate Pastor	8,000		
		44,850	
Mission			
10% of Fixed Costs	12,850		
20% of Head of Staff	16,000		
Budget Line Item	100,000		
		128,850	
Total Budget			530,000

FIGURE 4.15 Cost Assignments

Of course, ABC is not meant to replace the traditional line-item budget. But it can give us a picture of our spending from another angle. And the fascinating thing about ABC is that we can rearrange the pieces of the puzzle in an infinite number of ways. My managerial accounting professor always told us, "There is no right answer to these problems. The only thing I want to see is the right methodology being used." Indeed, as one example of how we can rearrange the data, we can pull the secretary's salary out of fixed costs, make a more refined breakdown of that position's time, and allocate those costs to various programs.

ABC offers the church two things. First, it breaks down the large line item of Salary and helps us see how those salaries (people!) are doing the work of the church. Second, it can help both pastors and personnel committees examine the way pastoral staff time is being used. I think ABC is too powerful a financial analysis tool to go unused in the church.

TIME SERIES TREND ANALYSIS

A basic technique for monitoring the financial life of an organization is to review performance over a period of years. This allows the financial management team to consider important trends that are developing. The trends may be positive or negative; either way, they need to be understood to manage properly the organization. In Figure 4.16 below, we can review the basic financials for Martin Luther Church laid out over a four-year period.

Trend Analysis 2007-2010

Revenue	2007	2008	2009	2010
Pledges	300,000	290,000	285,000	300,000
Open Plate	26,000	26,000	25,000	20,000
Friends	50,000	35,000	40,000	30,000
Special Gifts	20,000	40,000	35,000	30,000
Building Use	45,000	60,000	80,000	90,000
Other	25,000	17,000	25,000	25,000
Total Revenue	**466,000**	**468,000**	**490,000**	**495,000**
Expenses				
Salaries & Benefits	200,000	220,000	250,000	270,000
Program	75,000	60,000	55,000	50,000
Benevolences	75,000	75,000	60,000	50,000
Utilities	35,000	40,000	45,000	45,000
Maintenance	20,000	25,000	30,000	30,000
Administration	30,000	35,000	40,000	40,000
Other	31,000	13,000	10,000	10,000
Total Expenses	**466,000**	**468,000**	**490,000**	**495,000**

FIGURE 4.16 Trend Analysis

The trend analysis helps us identify a number of disturbing financial issues with which the leadership of Martin Luther Church needs to grapple. First, they are not growing their pledge revenue. Instead, they are growing their building use money. Given their dependence on that revenue stream, what happens if they lose the building users?

Second, as happens often in today's economy, the expenses for salary and benefits are growing faster than the revenue side of the budget. As a result, programs, and benevolences are being reduced to balance the budget. Won't this ultimately cause members to leave, creating additional revenue problems?

This type of analysis can be used for more discrete areas. For example, a congregation might want to examine specific expense areas such as maintenance, administration, or utilities. It is also essential for budget forecasting.

Congregations not employing trend analysis are missing one of the most valuable tools accounting can offer us. Too often, I think we avoid trend analysis because we are afraid the results will be negative. But not using it virtually guarantees negative long-term results for the ministry. We need the courage to compare where we are today with where we were in the past. We put ourselves in jeopardy by failing to do so.

FORECASTING FOR BUILDING A BUDGET

In addition to helping us understand what we've been spending, good financial records enable us to predict more accurately what revenue and expense will be in the future. They create the data for solid financial forecasting. Too few congregations forecast revenue and expense in any systematic manner. Why? Because many churches don't keep good enough financial records to make accurate forecasts.

Of course, forecasting assumes current and future financial performance will in some way resemble the past. There is no guarantee that this will be true. However, in most congregations, this is a very safe assumption. It is very rare that giving or spending varies radically from year to year.

I once did a statistical regression of the open plate giving for our congregation from year to year. Since open plate is usually dependent on the giving of visitors, I thought the statistical difference would be significant. I assumed that when there are more people in attendance at worship, the open plate would be higher. It wasn't. It turns out it matters more who is giving on any one Sunday than how many are giving. One large gift can change the figures more than a lot of small gifts. Even this seeming wild card was very consistent.

Certainly there are unusual events that can make revenue difficult to predict. A person can die and leave a congregation a huge bequest. Key members might move to another city and not pay the remaining balance on their pledge. Attendance may drop for inexplicable reasons (certainly not because of the preaching!), causing the open-plate collections to drop as well.

However, analysis of past revenue in a congregation usually reveals some very predictable patterns regarding revenue. First, patterns will emerge as to *when* people pay their pledges or tithes. Some congregations find that people are very steady in paying their pledges each month. Other congregations may discover they receive as much as 50 percent of their pledged income in the last two months of the year.

Second, the percentage of pledges that are actually paid tends to remain fairly constant in any given congregation. If $100,000 was pledged last year and $95,000 received, the 95 percent pay-up rate is a good indicator of what the congregation can expect in the year ahead. The further back in time a church can go to determine the percentage of pledges paid, the more accurate this predictor will be. Of course, if the congregation is growing and attracting many new members, different giving patterns may emerge. But the key is that *patterns* will emerge.

Open-plate giving usually has a close correlation with annual attendance. If a congregation received $25,000 with an average attendance of 170, it can generally expect the same amount in the coming year if attendance remains the same. Again, the more previous data one can incorporate into forecasts, the more likely they are to be accurate. Endowment growth, building use, and other sources of revenue can also be forecast using historical patterns.

Budget forecasting requires homework. A member of the finance committee can be assigned to talk with local utility companies about their expected rates for the upcoming year. Another member might talk with the insurance company about what it expects to charge.

One final issue about forecasting and budget building has to do with how one treats underspent line items. For example, if the Christian education committee has a budget of $5,000 but only spends $3,500, too often the response of the budget committee is, "Well, since they didn't need all their money this year, we will give them less money next year." In my opinion, this is very dangerous thinking. Once committees understand that budgets are being defined by this logic, they will spend all their money, whether they need to spend it or not, simply to ensure that their budget isn't reduced in the year ahead.

Instead of penalizing a committee for not spending all its funds, a better approach is for congregations to trust their committees. I know this is a radical approach for the church that proclaims God's trust of us. But trust does work! Ask committees what they need and, if the funds are available and the proposed expenditures align with the objectives and strategies of the congregation, give it to them.

FORECASTING CASH FLOW

It is extremely helpful for congregations to know *when* they receive revenue. If a congregation develops an accurate forecast of its cash flow, the treasurer can keep an adequate cash supply to meet current expenses, while not keeping too much money on hand. Too much money in the checking account means lost interest revenue in the savings account. In like manner, the actual draw down for expenses in past years can be used to create fairly accurate estimates for otherwise difficult categories such as utilities, office supplies, and telephones. It is possible to track when expenses are incurred. Items such as insurance payments and benevolence budget payouts are rather predictable.

Once past revenue and expense data has been entered into a program such as Excel, the flow of expenses can be shown on one graph while another graph displays the flow of revenue. The results are often startling, and can be of tremendous help to the treasurer in managing cash flow.

UNDERSTANDING THE OPPORTUNITY COST OF MONEY

Slightly more difficult than accounting but very important to church financial management is a basic financial concept called "the time value of money." This concept helps us understand the relationship between the present and future value of money. For example, if we invest $1,000 and assume it will earn 6 percent annually over the next ten years, the future value of that money, in today's dollars, is $1,791.

Why is this important? Our congregation's endowment is an example. If we withdraw $400,000 from the endowment to fund mission projects this year, we have spent $400,000, correct? Yes and no. We've spent $400,000 if we limit our vision to the present value of the money. But what if, instead of spending the $400,000, we invest it for, say, ten years at 6 percent (less 3 percent for annual inflation)? With the compounding effect of interest, the $400,000 at 3 percent (6 percent less 3 percent) is worth $537,566 (inflation adjusted) in ten years. The difference between the present and future value of the money is $137,566.

In business, the difference between present and future value of money is called the *opportunity cost of capital*. The future value is what it "costs" to use money today for a specific opportunity rather than invest it. A business assumes that, for any new venture to be worthwhile, it must at least cover the cost of its capital. The actual cost of our congregation's using the money today is not $400,000. It is the inflation adjusted $537,566 we would possess at the end of ten years if we left the money invested.

Of course, one might contend, "If the stock market goes down, we won't get 6 percent." Good point. That's why many prefer to use treasury bills as the safest and most reliable guide for future return. If a congregation can purchase 10-year treasury bills with a 4 percent return, still assuming a 3 percent inflation rate, the rate of return is 1 percent, which produces a future value of $441,488. The difference between the future value and the present value is $41,488. The rate of treasury bills minus inflation is the most conservative estimate of the opportunity cost of capital.

Another question concerns what timeline we use when determining cost of capital. How far out do we want to project the costs? Given the challenges of projecting financials, something in the 5–10 year frame is probably best.

Understanding the full implications of the present and future value of money is crucial. Even if the cost of capital is high, we may decide the mission of the church requires the use of a certain amount of money. Our rationale would be that the cost of capital is outweighed by the rewards we will reap by using the money in mission. Or we may decide that the proposed project, while it might be worth $400,000 today, is not worth the additional cost of the money we will lose by spending it now.

Understanding the present and future value of money can also help us manage our use of money internally. For example, our congregation sets aside $50,000 annually to a reserve fund for capital improvements. If we put the $50,000 in the reserve fund at the beginning of the year, it will be worth $50,000 plus interest at the end of the year. If we transfer the $50,000 at the end of the year, it will be worth $50,000. Some say, "So what? It isn't that big a difference." But that "So what?" is why businesses are usually better stewards of their money than are we in the church! Why do banks make mortgages due at the *beginning* of the month yet pay us interest at the *end* of the month? It is that "So what?" Interest adds up. Whenever a congregation's money is earning interest rather than being expended, it provides additional money for future mission.

AUDITING

In light of the scandals at Enron, brokerage firms, and elsewhere, people are now keenly aware of the need for proper auditing in corporations. A church is no different. Unfortunately, churches experience a huge amount of fraud and theft. Equally troubling is the use of funds for reasons not reflected in the budget.

One of the most troubling financial practices in too many churches involves "off the books" money coming in and going out. These funds are never recorded in any formal account. It usually passes through a transfer account. A classic example is when a church member wants to fund a special music project. He or she gives the money, and it is spent directly on the music. However, the gift never appears as designated cash received or as an expense in the music account.

Practices like this can get church leaders in trouble. Every dollar received by a church should be recorded in an account in the books. In this case the revenue should be recorded as a designated gift, perhaps as a designated gift for music. (A new line item may have to be created to identify the gift.) In like manner, the expense needs to be recorded, perhaps in a line item marked special music.

By adopting a transparent methodology, there will be no one standing up at the congregation's annual meeting saying, "How did we pay for that special music? Where did the money come from?" Show people the sources of revenue and expense and the congregation will have total confidence in the financial management. Hide or fail to account for some revenue or expense and people will begin to suspect that someone is playing financial games—and they're right!

A full audit is expensive and usually is not legally required for a congregation's financial operations. Most congregations buy something called a "review." A review involves auditors doing many of the same financial checks but doesn't require that they put their findings into as significant a legally binding letter as a full audit does. Less liability equals less cost!

Finding an auditor for congregational purposes can be a challenge. Auditors who specialize in business work are expensive. Auditors who understand church finances are not so readily available. I recommend speaking with other congregations to find out which auditors they use, how much they charge, and how responsive they are during the year as questions arise. As with any other hire, it is important to have the auditors be interviewed by members who can ask the right questions.

Systemic Issues

Finances cannot be viewed solely in terms of dollars and cents. There are deeply embedded emotional issues in the life of each congregational system that shape how financial issues are approached and handled. For example, Western was almost bankrupt twice in our 155-year history. As a result, even though Western has significant financial reserves today, the congregation has what I consider to be an inappropriate anxiety level that it will end up near bankruptcy again.

It's important that all major decision-makers in the management of a congregation's finances understand the financial history of the system. This includes the church governing board, finance committee, and staff. For example, if there is a history of financial data not being transparent, it is nearly impossible for the current leaders to be *too* transparent.

A congregational system also needs a blend of continuity and new faces. It takes a while to understand a congregation's finances. So the treasurer position should be held by someone willing to stick with the job for five years or so. Similarly, a majority of the finance committee should have been around for a while. But there needs to be some degree of turnover lest the congregation think finances are the turf of a small group. Furthermore, new eyes are more likely to spot fraud or mistakes than those who have been looking at the financial system for years.

THE FINANCE COMMITTEE

Lay leadership in the areas of finances is usually assigned to a church treasurer working with a finance committee or board of trustees. It is important for these leaders to have carefully defined descriptions of their role. If the task is too broad, it will create anger in other committees and church's elected governing body. The committee may begin to assume powers that are constitutionally assigned to the primary governing body. If the role description is too narrow, it will lead to inadequate and uncreative financial management. The committee will not feel empowered to ask questions and raise issues.

Constitutionally, the elected officers of a congregation are normally the individuals charged with deciding how money is spent—when, where, and on what. They are the "vision group" that's charged with linking budget resources to the goals and objectives the congregation has established. They have the broadest perspective and base of information to decide how funds are expended.

The role of any finance committee is to provide the elected officers (and the congregation) and staff, the "vision group" as it were, with the data and material they need to make informed decisions. Therefore, the committee should provide the elected officers with regular financial statements, assessments of how investments are performing, and short- and long-term trend information. Has pledging been going up or down over the past five years? Are building costs rising and, if yes, why? If the finance committee senses that a certain ministry strategy puts the financial position of the church at risk, they should speak up.

However, the role of the finance committee is not to decide where budget cuts or increases should be made. Indeed, in my opinion, this shouldn't even be a subject for discussion in the finance committee. If it is, the committee will no longer be viewed as an objective presenter of information. Rather, any and all budget suggestions the committee makes will be viewed as having an agenda behind them.

I have seen churches where the finance committee or board of trustees have equal power with the congregation's primary governing body. I have never seen such a two-headed system be productive. It inevitably leads to division—with charges of "lack of fiscal responsibility" aimed at the governing board and charges of "lack of vision" aimed at the finance people.

Carefully defined roles for the people in charge of financial leadership are crucial. Defining these roles will lead to healthy debates over finances versus power struggles between boards and committees. Perhaps this is why Paul urged the Corinthians to have those with the gift of administration administrate while letting teachers teach and prophets prophesy (1 Cor. 12:27–31). The finance committee should contain people who know how to present financial information verbally and in print. Graphs, charts, data tables, and many other tools are available in accounting software as well as Excel. These can be used to help members better understand the financial situation of the congregation.

Finally, the finance committee is responsible for setting up "best practices" for handling money so the congregation isn't the victim of fraud or theft. These best practices can be developed by consulting with other congregations. For example, most congregations insist on two counters being present to count any incoming cash (to avoid money being stolen before it is accounted for); require more than one signature for checks over a certain size; have multiple people approving vouchers to authorize disbursements (to prevent an employee or treasurer from authorizing disbursements to him- or herself); and have more than one set of eyes looking at the reconciliation of bank statements (to insure vouchers and disbursements match and no unauthorized disbursement is made).

BEYOND A "FAITH-BASED" APPROACH TO MONEY

I have heard many stories of pastors telling their congregations they need to go into debt or stretch themselves financially as "a matter of faith." The pastor stands up and challenges the congregation to have the faith that "God will provide." Such statements suggest that those who do not go along with a particular financial proposal lack faith. I find this approach enraging and theologically false.

A church member who questions a particular use of funds, or who takes a conservative approach to financial issues, is not showing a lack of faith. She or he is simply asking a very basic question: "How are we going to pay for this?" Similarly, a member who wants to build up the congregation's endowment fund is not necessarily advocating that the church stockpile money while the world is ravaged by hunger and disease. He or she may see a strong endowment as an instrument to alleviate hunger and disease in the future as well as the present.

These values attached to certain financial strategies get implanted in congregational systems over a period of time. As a result, they implicitly yet firmly shape the nature of all conversations about finances. Managers may not be able to deal with the "numbers" until they deal with these deeper issues.

To frame financial issues as expressions of faith (or lack of faith) grossly distorts the values and issues being discussed. It makes the mission-oriented person appear to be fiscally irresponsible while the appropriately cautious budget person comes across as opposed to mission. We simply have to stop this caricaturing of one another.

As I've said, the church has much it can learn from the business community. Most every company is trying to make money. Some companies are run on conservative financial principles while others are run on very risk-embracing financial strategies. Yet all business strategies have to be justified on the basis of how much they cost, how they will impact the well-being of the company, and how they further the strategic goals of the company. There is absolutely no reason why the church shouldn't do the same.

Surely, there will be times when a congregation adopts more of a risk-taking approach to the use of its financial resources. However, it must be a well calculated risk. The issue is not faith *per se*. The issue is whether a particular use of a congregation's financial resources is appropriate, given the realities of the congregation's situation. Do the things that will be accomplished by the expenditure of funds warrant the risk that spending the funds will incur?

When making financial decisions, a congregation needs to have a vision, objectives that will help translate the vision into reality, strategies to accomplish the objectives, and measurements that will allow the congregation to evaluate progress or lack of progress on the strategies. In the planning process, a governing body can begin to assign price tags to the various components of the ministry plan—allowing it to compare option A with option B, and make other strategic calculations.

Perhaps a congregation is considering an aggressive advertising or public relations campaign to help grow its membership. After designing a public relations strategy, the church calculates that the cost will be $50,000 annually for the next three years. Is it a "lack of faith" to question that expense? Is it a lack of faith to prefer the money be spent on a health clinic in Ethiopia? Is it a lack of faith to suggest the money should be invested for the next three years so that it will produce a gain that will enable even more ministry to be done? I don't think so. These are matters of ministry strategy.

Financial decisions are nothing more or less than choices between competing priorities. A congregation should welcome such debates. They've been taking place since Peter and Paul slugged it out over whether taking the gospel to the Gentiles was a good investment of resources! Why should we be any different? I wouldn't want to be a part of a congregation whose members don't feel passionate about how money is used for ministry. Nonetheless, when debating competing values and priorities, it simply is not helpful to describe some values as faithful and others as not faithful.

A conservative approach can protect and build tremendous resources for future generations to engage in ministry. As mentioned earlier, my congregation puts $50,000 a year into a capital improvements fund. We decided to do this after conducting a detailed building management analysis that looked at *what* we will need to replace in the building and *when*. Our analysis determined that we need to set aside $50,000 annually to ensure that the building is maintained.

Periodically someone asks, "Why are we putting all that money aside when we could use it for mission projects?" Our response is that by maintaining the building today, a future generation won't have to take $100,000 away from its mission funds to replace a boiler or air-handling unit. Are we right? I think so. But I don't think the people who question our policy are wrong or lack faith! They simply approach the issue from a different perspective and reach different conclusions.

FUNDRAISING

I don't remember any of my seminary professors talking about the crucial role I would play as a pastor in fundraising. However, managing the process of fundraising absorbs a lot of any pastor's time. Worse, I don't remember anybody telling me that if I failed at managing fundraising, staff members could lose their jobs and important ministries might have to be terminated.

Fundraising is not about money. It is about ministry. No doubt this explains, in part, why Jesus talked so much about money and stewardship.

I know many ministers who adopt the attitude "Funding the ministry is the responsibility of the laity." However, does the head of a university feel no obligation to see that sufficient funds exist for students to be educated and faculty and staff paid? Does the head of a nonprofit housing corporation feel no obligation to ensure that funds are raised so poor people can be placed in decent housing and staff salaries paid?

Indeed, it is the responsibility of the laity to fund the ministry. It is also their responsibility to make sure God is worshipped, believers are educated, and mission work is done. We clergy don't run from responsibility in these other areas. Why do so many of us run away from the subject of fundraising?

There is no question in my mind that lay-led fundraising efforts are more effective than those dominated by clergy. However, good fundraising requires an understanding of the people from whom funds will be solicited. Theoretically, the pastor knows the congregation better than anyone; so her or his advice, in this respect, is invaluable. Furthermore, there are some people who want to talk to the pastor about their giving. They may have complaints or new ideas—or perhaps they just feel better if they have a chance to sit down with the pastor and discuss how much they are giving and why.

As we think about fundraising, it's important to realize the entire area of designated giving is controversial. To go back to a previous example, a member may want to make a special musical event happen. Should we allow her to fund that specific project? I don't think there is a right or wrong answer. I do know that most of us tend to be against special giving when it supports something we don't necessarily support. We tend to be somewhat less judgmental when the special giving supports an area we highly value. But whether we tend to favor designated giving or not, our ministries will most likely be hampered by a lack of funds until we know the methods and master the skills of managing fundraising.

Not "Worldly" But Faithful

Accounting and finance issues, various strategies and approaches toward the use of money, presentations of financial information—none of these are terribly complex. So why do most clergy and churches do them so poorly? I think we have a theologically rooted problem with money. We think money is dirty. We are concerned that we will be compromised by things financial. And yet, Jesus spoke about money more than any other topic. He didn't always use the word *money*. However, he talked frequently about the management of financial resources.

Managing and increasing the assets of the church is not a "worldly" thing to do. As the parable of the pounds shows, it is a faithful thing to do. Until we rid ourselves of this notion that money and everything about it is "nonspiritual" or a temptation, we will continue to waste opportunities to maximize the resources God has given us for ministry.

A Manager's Checklist

- Do internal audits *during* the year, not just once at the end of the year. Members of the finance committee can perform an ongoing auditing function by checking a number of randomly selected items to make sure vouchers match entries, money is credited to the correct accounts, and other basic accounting functions are performed correctly. This ensures that bills are being paid in a timely manner and being recorded accurately.
- Communicate well and frequently. A manager doesn't do all the accounting work. However, good managers make sure financial information is clearly formatted and regularly made available to the congregation.
- In order for a pastor to be an effective manager, he or she needs to be involved in the meetings and activities of those responsible for the financial life of the congregation. When

this happens, the people handling money know the pastor, as a manager, is interested, supportive, and knowledgeable.

- Look closely at the financial reports that are produced. If something is unclear, ask questions. Managers cannot manage what they don't understand.

- Transparency, transparency, transparency. Make all financial data available to the congregation and committees in a timely manner. When there is a problem, managers need to gather all the information on the situation and bring it to the proper body. Excellent managers work collaboratively to solve financial problems.

- Make sure responsibilities to the government are covered. Forgiveness is a theological concept, not an IRS concept. For example, if a payment for tax and social security withholding to the Internal Revenue Service is late or wrong, the penalty is *on the entire amount* of the deposit (not just that amount of the error). In other words, if a $5,000 payment due to the IRS is too little by $10, the penalty interest is assessed against the $5,000 not the $10.

- For those readers who read the T-account and Journal Entry section of this chapter, there are some simple accounting exercises to be found in appendix C. Please take a few minutes to test your growing knowledge!

conclusion

Congregational Management: A Holy Calling

C ongregations are among the most fascinating systems anyone can be called to manage. Like all systems, they are filled with anxiety. Unlike most systems, they also are filled with a peace the world cannot give. Like most systems, they are guided by a vision. Unlike most systems, they are guided by a vision that has endured for two thousand years. As managers of these congregational systems, we make a mistake if we ignore the God-given vision and divinely implanted peace that has sustained the Christian church and congregational life for two millennia. They are strengths upon which we can build effective, growing ministries.

To fully maximize the vision and allow the peace of Christ to manifest itself in the lives of congregations, managers need to pay close attention to the systemic inputs of people, facilities, and money that generate the ministry outputs God calls on congregations to produce. To that end, we have detailed how management is involved in congregations:

- *Thinking Systemically.* When managers of congregations deal solely with parts of the body of Christ rather than the whole, they become totally reactive. They fix the plumbing leak but never address an aging plumbing system that, over time, will deplete scarce financial resources that could have been used for mission. Reactive managing is more time-consuming than proactive attention to the system as a whole. When a major personnel, facilities, or financial sub-system malfunctions, it can bring the entire congregation to a grinding halt. It is far easier to keep a system maintained and running properly than to restore one that has failed. But such care requires that managers recognize and understand the systems of which they are stewards. To stay focused on the relationship of the parts and the whole, I recommend keeping Paul's body of Christ imagery front and center. Comparing the body of Christ and it parts with the human body and its parts, Paul blends the idea of the whole with its parts in pure system theory manner. Just as the human body needs ears as well as eyes, the body of Christ needs teachers, prophets, leaders, and managers. This is not only excellent theology. It is also excellent management theory.

- *Understanding the Difference Between Management and Leadership.* Effective organizations are run by people who know when they are leading and when they are managing. The two require very different but complementary ways of thinking. Leadership thinks long-term, management short-term; leadership focuses on strategic issues, management on implementation; leadership inspires people, manage-ment brings people together into a cohesive, efficient group. When a pastor or layperson can differentiate between those occasions when she needs to lead and those when she needs to manage, she will be more effective and fulfilled.

- *Lubricating the System.* Managers "grease the gears" of a system to keep it running smoothly. Before friction (such as facilities issues, personnel problems, or financial surprises) reaches the point where it can limit ministry, managers apply the needed lubrication (usually involving more people, space, or money) to keep the parts running smoothly. If the system lacks effective management, the parts will begin to work against themselves in ways that damage the productivity of the whole. Paul advises that even the most nondescript parts of the body of Christ are significant. So it is in the life of a congregation.

- *Maximizing the Possibilities of the Parts.* When working with personnel, effective managers seek to bring out the best in those they manage while limiting the impact of an employee's weaknesses on the system. With facilities, managers make the most of the limited space they manage, setting aside funds to pay for future capital costs. With finances, managers maximize dollars by ensuring that money is handled in a manner that discourages fraud, keeping utility and insurance costs as low as possible, and matching investments appropriately to the needs of the congregation.

- *Limiting Risks.* By the nature of their role in a system, congregational *leaders* are supposed to take appropriate risks. They may choose to start a program for which there is, initially, inadequate personnel and financial inputs. Fulfilling their role, congregational *managers* are supposed to identify and reduce risks. They ask the questions the dreamers sometimes ignore: "How are we going to pay for this?" or "Are we ready to make the repairs and renovations to our electrical and plumbing systems that will be needed to sustain this new program?

- *Aligning the Parts.* Productive managers have a clear understanding of the vision and goals a congregation is attempting to implement. Ideally, this vision has been mapped out in a strategic plan that includes accompanying objectives, strategies, and performance measures. When the inputs of facilities, finance, and people are aligned with a well-thought-out strategic plan grounded in solid theology, a congregation can move mountains. However, it's essential to have every part of the body aligned and invested in the plan. The organization's "foot" needs to understand that it is as important as the "brain." As Harvard Business School's Kim Clark says, "You need to have everybody believe in the organization. You need everybody to think that they're part of it, and they are being invested in, as well as being asked of."[1]

The best managers learn as they manage. Sometimes, we learn more from our mistakes than our successes. However, learning what works and doesn't work with our given inputs and our own individual strengths and weaknesses as managers is key to growing into the practice of management.

Henry Mintzberg is a professor of managerial studies at McGill University whose writings are filled with great wisdom as well as practical insights. In his latest book, *Managing*, he writes, "Let's recognize management as a *calling*, and so appreciate that efforts to professionalize it, and turn it into a science, undermine that calling."[2] I couldn't agree more. Management is a calling—and managing a congregation is a holy calling. Good managers help God and God's people do God's work. It is my hope and prayer that this book has added a bit to the conversation about management in the church, and that the discussion will grow in the years ahead.

A Sample Balance Sheet

A balance sheet is a "snapshot" of a congregation's assets and liabilities at a particular point in time. The accumulated depreciation numbers can be helpful in understanding the value of furniture and equipment, though they are less helpful with real estate, which often appreciates rather than depreciates. On the asset side of a balance sheet, the "liquid" assets are most important (cash, stocks, and bonds) because they can be used for ministry when needed. The value of fixed assets is usually important only if a congregation is willing to sell the asset.

Central Church
Balance Sheet
December 31, 2009

ASSETS		
Current Assets		
Checking/Savings		
Petty Cash		500.00
Wachovia Bank		
Checking Account		419.74
Money Market Account		24,213.37
Total Wachovia Bank		24,633.11
Total Checking/Savings		25,133.11

Other Current Assets		
Due from Building Users	2,108.14	
Loans	750.00	
Total Other Current Assets	2,858.14	
Total Current Assets		27,991.25
Fixed Assets		
Cemetery Plots	14,400.00	
Church		
Building		
Acc Depreciation	-1,879,987.50	
Building - Other	5,898,000.00	
Total Building	4,018,012.50	
Furniture & Equipment		
Acc Depreciation	-253,095.04	
Furniture & Equipment - Other	438,573.56	
Total Furniture & Equipment	185,478.52	
Land	10,000,000.00	
Total Church	14,203,491.02	
Manse		
Building		
Acc Depreciation	-118,401.87	
Building - Other	287,491.75	
Total Building	169,089.88	
Furn & Equip - Manse	3,171.89	
Land	132,250.00	
Total Manse	304,511.77	
Total Fixed Assets		14,522,402.79
Other Assets		
Endowment		
Shared Equity Property	200,000.00	
Cash Equivalents		
US Govt.	135,772.44	
Corporate Bonds		
Total Corporate Bonds	229,375.00	
Equities	2,115,502.89	
Municipal Bonds	229,502.65	
Preferred Equities	432,008.50	
Total Endowment	3,342,161.48	
Capital Reserve Fund		
Cash Equivalents/Reserve		
U.S. Govt. Fund	267,495.83	
Equities	10,199.06	
Total Capital Reserve Fund	277,694.89	
Total Other Assets		3,619,856.37
TOTAL ASSETS		**18,170,250.41**
LIABILITIES & EQUITY		
Liabilities		
Current Liabilities		
Other Current Liabilities		
2009 Prepayments	4,893.00	
Direct Deposit Liabilities	-26,239.97	

Payroll Liabilities		
Advance		
Employee	1,424.23	
Advance - Other	-824.23	
Total Advance	600.00	
Annuity		
403-B Contributions (Equitable)	-1,321.56	
Total Annuity	-1,321.56	
Dental Insurance	49.00	
FICA		
Company	-363.39	
Total FICA	-363.39	
Medicare		
Company	-84.99	
Total Medicare	-84.99	
Payroll Liabilities - Other	416.19	
Total Payroll Liabilities	-704.75	
Security Card Deposits	2,545.00	
Total Other Current Liabilities	-19,506.72	
Total Current Liabilities	-19,506.72	
Total Liabilities		-19,506.72
Equity		
Retained Earnings	174,764,556.18	
Wachovia/Restricted		
Money Market Account		
Camp Funds (Escrow)	13.89	
Building Improvement Reserve	12,733.09	
Endowment	-35,783.57	
Special Benevolence	2,445.05	
Memorials (Undesignated)	1,221.42	
Prison Ministry	420.00	
Replacement Reserve	537,870.54	
Special Gifts/Assoc Pastor	236.81	
Special Gifts/Head of Staff	5,617.66	
Total Money Market Account	524,774.89	
Total Wachovia/Restricted	524,774.89	
Net Income	-99,573.94	
Total Equity		18,189,757.13
TOTAL LIABILITIES & EQUITY		**18,170,250.41**

A Sample
Income Statement

A n income statement gives a congregation's governing body a lot of information. It allows the officers to evaluate year-to-date revenue and expenses, see what percentage of any line item has been received or spent, and examine the differences in the current and prior year budgets. The year-to-date difference in various line items is probably the most important information. Bills tend to get paid in the same sequence year after year. Insurance bills are paid on similar dates, salaries are paid out over the same pay intervals, and heating and cooling costs tends to increase in the same months each year. Thus, the year-to-date numbers are much more helpful than the percent of the budget spent.

Income Statement
Jan-Nov 2009

	Revised 2008 Budget	Jan-Nov 2008	2009 Session-Approved Revised Budget*	Jan-Nov 2009	Difference 2009 vs. 2008 (Actual)	Percent of Budget (2009)
REVENUE						
Revenue-Members & Friends						
Flower Fund	11,000.00	16,021.74	10,000.00	0.00	-16,021.74	0.00%
Fundraising Event	2,500.00	2,119.80	2,250.00	2,782.00	662.20	123.64%
Initial Offering	0.00	0.00	7,000.00	6,586.00	6,586.00	94.09%
Nonpledging Income	100.00	96.00	100.00	151.00	55.00	151.00%
Open Plate	8,000.00	2,585.00	9,000.00	7,125.00	4,540.00	79.17%
Per Capita	27,000.00	31,145.52	29,000.00	26,157.00	-4,988.52	90.20%
Pledges-Designated (Prior Year)	1,000.00	1,559.00	1,500.00	1,937.00	378.00	129.13%
Pledges-Designated-Benevolences	1,000.00	485.00	200.00	2,735.00	2,250.00	1367.50%
Pledges-Designated-Benevolences	220.00	220.00	220.00	220.00	0.00	100.00%
Pledges-Designated-Church Door	220.00	220.00	220.00	220.00	0.00	100.00%
Pledges-Designated-Expenses	160.00	160.00	160.00	160.00	0.00	100.00%
Pledges-Envelopes-Undesignated (12/31/08)	1,380.00	1,380.00	1,380.00	1,420.00	40.00	102.90%
Pledges-Envelopes-Undesignated (01/01/09→)	559,018.00	550,110.00	570,000.00	520,000.00	-30,110.00	89.66%
Pledges-Undesignated-New Members	8,300.00	8,860.00	10,000.00	2,340.00	-6,520.00	31.20%
Revenue-Members & Friends (Subtotal)	627,178.00	614,742.06	648,310.00	571,613.00	-43,129.06	98.02%
Revenue-Other						
Endowment Draw (Operations)	175,000.00	165,000.00	125,000.00	138,725.00	-26,275.00	110.98%
Endowment Draw (Capital Reserve)	50,000.00	42,000.00	50,000.00	45,000.00	3,000.00	90.00%
Copier Use Reimbursement	3,100.00	3,800.83	4,000.00	3,952.32	151.49	98.81%
Interest Income/Money Market Account	100.00	178.10	75.00	23.50	-154.60	31.33%
Daycare Program (Use of Facilities)	0.00	0.00	42,000.00	35,000.00	35,000.00	83.33%
Miscellaneous	0.00	0.00	0.00	0.00	0.00	0.00%
Use of Facilities	16,000.00	13,400.00	17,000.00	14,450.00	1,050.00	85.00%
Revenue-Other (Subtotal)	244,200.00	224,378.93	238,075.00	237,150.82	12,771.89	99.61%
TOTAL REVENUE	871,378.00	839,120.99	886,385.00	808,763.82	-30,357.17	91.24%

EXPENSES

Personnel

Salaries	245,814.00	231,919.92	257,614.00	238,261.90	6,341.98	92.49%
Benefits	184,100.00	169,351.31	192,900.00	178,155.22	8,803.91	92.36%
Salaries & Benefits (Subtotal)	429,914.00	401,271.23	450,514.00	416,417.12	15,145.89	92.43%

Administration

Accounting Review & Services	6,500.00	6,500.00	7,400.00	7,249.00	749.00	97.96%
Advertising	8,000.00	6,195.71	2,400.00	2,131.56	-4,064.15	88.82%
Bank Service/Wire Transfer Fees	25.00	149.79	600.00	571.56	421.77	95.26%
Contingency	600.00	0.00	500.00	0.00	0.00	0.00%
Copier & Computer Supplies	800.00	516.43	700.00	65.97	-450.46	9.42%
Copier Usage	6,000.00	5,766.17	7,000.00	6,313.92	547.75	90.20%
Cyber/Web Site Development	1,000.00	1,685.95	1,000.00	400.22	-1,285.73	40.02%
DSL Service	2,200.00	1,979.45	2,200.00	2,159.40	179.95	98.15%
Office Equipment-Maintenance	2,500.00	2,863.30	3,000.00	2,792.09	-71.21	93.07%
Office Equipment-Purchase	1,000.00	430.96	1,000.00	-202.00	-632.96	-20.20%
Office Equipment-Lease	8,000.00	6,798.78	7,500.00	6,609.26	-189.52	88.12%
Office Supplies & Printing	4,300.00	4,484.81	7,500.00	6,810.94	2,326.13	90.81%
Per Capita	7,500.00	7,500.00	8,060.00	8,060.00	560.00	100.00%
Personnel/Administration	750.00	675.00	750.00	675.00	0.00	90.00%
Postage/Shipping	2,300.00	2,433.51	3,000.00	2,003.56	-429.95	66.79%
Publications/Subscriptions	0.00	200.90	100.00	0.00	-200.90	0.00%
Staff Training/Development	250.00	0.00	250.00	0.00	0.00	0.00%
Telephone	5,600.00	5,099.74	6,500.00	5,397.47	297.73	83.04%
Administration (Subtotal)	57,325.00	53,280.50	59,460.00	51,037.95	-2,242.55	85.84%

Plant and Property Operations

Building Engineering Services	11,750.00	10,416.00	12,000.00	10,472.00	56.00	87.27%
Capital Reserve Fund	50,000.00	45,000.00	50,000.00	45,000.00	0.00	90.00%
Electricity	58,000.00	55,959.39	55,000.00	50,884.97	-5,074.42	92.52%
Equipment & Furnishings/Purchase	500.00	222.45	1,000.00	720.11	497.66	72.01%
Gas	12,000.00	11,373.75	12,000.00	11,886.70	512.95	99.06%
Insurance	35,000.00	29,510.00	32,000.00	29,149.58	-360.42	91.09%
Insurance Offset (Miriam's Kitchen)	-5,500.00	-8,287.25	-7,700.00	-8,287.25	0.00	107.63%

Maintenance-Church	24,000.00	17,347.31	20,000.00	18,166.64	819.33	90.83%
Maintenance-Manse	500.00	129.50	1,000.00	129.50	0.00	12.95%
Service Contracts	14,500.00	11,766.03	13,000.00	12,201.72	435.69	93.86%
Supplies	8,000.00	6,311.50	7,000.00	6,637.95	326.45	94.83%
Taxes-Church Rental Property	8,500.00	8,037.08	9,000.00	8,037.08	0.00	89.30%
Van Maintenance	1,500.00	627.01	2,500.00	1,944.86	1,317.85	77.79%
Water Service	6,700.00	6,745.69	7,800.00	6,981.61	235.92	89.51%
Plant and Property (Subtotal)	225,450.00	195,158.46	214,600.00	193,925.47	-1,232.99	90.37%
Ministry						
Campus Ministry						
Alternative Spring Break (Contribution)	0.00	0.00	0.00	0.00	0.00	0.00%
Choir Scholarships	2,400.00	1,200.00	2,000.00	1,800.00	600.00	90.00%
Conferences/Miscellaneous	500.00	0.00	0.00	0.00	0.00	
Meals/Brunches	3,000.00	2,500.00	3,000.00	2,800.00	300.00	93.33%
Printing/Publications/Advertising	5,000.00	5,000.00	5,000.00	4,500.00	-500.00	
Program General	3,800.00	2,870.30	3,800.00	3,600.00	729.70	
Campus Ministry (Subtotal)	14,700.00	11,570.30	13,800.00	12,700.00	1,129.70	92.03%
Christian Education						
Adult Education & Materials	200.00	184.76	0.00	12.00	-172.76	
Children & Youth Education	7,000.00	6,500.00	7,000.00	6,000.00	-500.00	85.71%
Director, Christian Education	3,000.00	2,590.00	15,000.00	12,000.00	9,410.00	80.00%
Special Activities	300.00	144.93	300.00	0.00	-144.93	0.00%
Christian Education (Subtotal)	10,500.00	9,419.69	22,300.00	18,012.00	8,592.31	80.77%
Congregational Ministry						
Laypersons & Officer Development	0.00	0.00	0.00	0.00	0.00	
Programs-Congregational	7,000.00	6,200.00	6,000.00	5,000.00	-1,200.00	83.33%
Congregational Ministry (Subtotal)	7,000.00	6,200.00	6,000.00	5,000.00	-1,200.00	83.33%
Deacons						
Annual Retreat/Picnic	1,000.00	133.53	200.00	183.05	49.52	91.53%
Congregational Benevolence Fund	2,000.00	880.00	1,300.00	51.50	-828.50	3.96%
Family & Friends	500.00	257.57	500.00	73.94	-183.63	14.79%
Fellowship & Community Building	1,000.00	420.74	800.00	59.29	-361.45	7.41%
Deacons (Subtotal)	4,500.00	1,691.84	2,800.00	367.78	-1,324.06	13.14%

Music					
Additional Paid Singers	850.00	300.00	425.00	150.00	-150.00	35.29%
Music & Supplies	600.00	139.10	200.00	31.45	-107.65	15.73%
Organ & Keyboard Maintenance	3,000.00	2,585.00	2,600.00	2,700.00	115.00	103.85%
Special Music	800.00	315.00	400.00	515.00	200.00	128.75%
Substitute Organists	1,800.00	1,650.00	1,500.00	1,100.00	-550.00	73.33%
Music (Subtotal)	7,050.00	4,989.10	5,125.00	4,496.45	-492.65	87.74%
Worship					
Worship-Guest Ministers	500.00	0.00	250.00	350.00	350.00	140.00%
Worship-Flowers	2,100.00	2,301.33	2,800.00	2,172.35	-128.98	77.58%
Worship-Supplies	650.00	2,291.95	650.00	334.54	-1,957.41	51.47%
Worship (Subtotal)	3,250.00	4,593.28	3,700.00	2,856.89	-1,736.39	77.21%
Ministry (Subtotal)	47,000.00	38,464.21	53,725.00	43,433.12	4,968.91	80.84%
Current Expenses (Subtotal)	759,689.00	688,174.40	778,299.00	704,813.66	16,639.26	90.56%
Benevolences	120,000.00	140,000.00	100,000.00	90,000.00	-50,000.00	90.00%
EXPENSES (TOTAL)	879,689.00	828,174.40	878,299.00	794,813.66	-33,360.74	90.49%
REVENUE OVER EXPENSE	-8,311.00	10,946.59	8,086.00	13,950.16	3,003.57	

Accounting Exercises

For those readers who were engaged by the accounting section of chapter 4, here are some simple exercises to test your understanding of some basic issues in accounting. You'll find the answers at the end of the section.

1. Label the following accounts as asset, liability, expense, or revenue accounts:

   a. Cash
   b. Utilities
   c. Mortgage
   d. Pledges
   e. Funds from Building Use
   f. Building and Grounds
   g. Salaries
   h. Benevolences
   i. IRS Withholding Monies
   j. Escrowed Continuing Education Money for the Pastor
   k. Christian Education Curriculum

2. Prepare journal and T-account entries for the following transaction: The secretary purchases $400 worth of postage.

3. Prepare journal and T-account entries for the following transaction: A member died and left the church a $25,000 bequest.

4. From the following list of accounts, prepare a balance sheet:

a. Mortgage Due	1,250,000
b. Cash on Hand	50,000
c. Building & Grounds	2,000,000
d. Endowment	450,000
e. IRS Withholding Monies	40,000
f. Memorial Funds	25,000

5. From the following list of accounts, prepare an income statement:

a. Pledges Received	50,000
b. Utilities	20,000
c. Salaries	50,000
d. Program	5,000
e. Draw on Endowment	20,000
f. Building Use Funds	3,000

Answers

1.
     a. Cash   Asset or Revenue
On the balance sheet cash is an asset; on the income statement it is a revenue account.
     b. Utilities   Expense

c. Mortgage   Liability
   Anything a congregation owes to another person or party is a liability.
d. Pledges   Asset or Revenue
   Pledges are an asset on the balance sheet and a revenue line item on the income statement.
e. Funds from Building Use   Revenue
f. Building and Grounds   Asset
g. Salaries   Expense
h. Benevolences   Expense
i. IRS Withholding Monies   Liability
   This money is taken from salaries, and is owed and paid to the IRS. Thus, while it inflates the cash on hand, it is a liability.
j. Escrowed Continuing Education
   Money for the Pastor   Liability
   Money owed to the pastor for continuing education that was not spent in the past period can't be carried forward into a new year without creating an escrow account that shows up on the balance sheet as a liability. If the pastor were to leave the congregation without using these funds, the liability would be eliminated from the balance sheet.
k. Christian Education Curriculum   Expense

2. Postage   400
       Cash   400

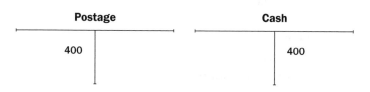

Note: Some congregations might refine this transaction with a Petty Cash account. In that case, one would take money from Petty Cash to pay the postage. Petty Cash, in turn, would need to be replenished periodically from the more general Cash account.

3. There are several ways to handle bequests. However, they all start with an entry that shows up on the income statement. The cash has to be received and assigned to a revenue account (I have assigned it to Endowment Revenue. In some congregations, the revenue account is entitled Bequests or Special Gifts). Once recorded in a revenue account, the congregation might transfer the revenue to an asset account such as an endowment or a designated asset account such as mission fund or music fund. It could also move the funds to an asset account and use the money for current expense.

Cash	25,000
Endowment Revenue	25,000

Endowment	Cash
25,000	25,000

4.

Assets		
Cash on Hand	50,000	
Building & Grounds	2,000,000	
Endowment	450,000	
Memorial Funds	25,000	
Total Assets		2,525,000
Liabilities		
Mortgage Due	1,250,000	
IRS Withholding Monies	40,000	
Total Liabilities		1,290,000
Net Worth		1,235,000

5.

Revenue
      Pledges Received   50,000
      Draw on Endowment   20,000
      Building Use Funds   3,000
      Total Revenue   73,000

Expense
      Utilities   20,000
      Salaries   50,000
      Program   5,000
Total Expense   75,000

Surplus (Deficit)   (2,000)

Notes

Introduction: The Ministry of Management

1. Floyd H. Flake, Elaine McCollins Flake, and Edwin C. Reed, *African American Church Management Handbook* (Valley Forge, PA: Judson Press, 2005).

2. Peter F. Drucker and Joseph A. Maciariello, *Management,* rev. ed. (New York: Collins, 2008), 23.

Chapter 1: Managing Congregational Systems

1. Edwin H. Friedman, *Generation to Generation: Family Process in Church and Synagogue* (New York: Guilford Press, 1985).

2. Peter Drucker, *Management,* rev. ed. (New York: Collins, 2008), 124.

3. John P. Kotter, *A Force for Change: How Leadership Differs from Management* (New York: Free Press, 1990), 5.

4. Kotter, *A Force for Change,* 7.

5. Thomas Peters and Robert Waterman, *In Search of Excellence: Lessons from America's Best Run Companies* (New York: HarperCollins, 1982).

6. Peter Senge, *The Fifth Discipline: The Art & Practice of the Learning Organization* (New York: Doubleday, 1990).

7. Arlin Rothauge, *Sizing Up a Congregation for New Member Ministry* (New York: Episcopal Church Center, 1983); Roy M. Oswald, "How to Minister Effectively in Family, Pastoral, Program, and Corporate-Sized Churches," *Action Information* 17, no. 2 (March/April 1991): 1–7; Alice Mann, *The In-Between Church: Navigating Size Transitions in Congregations* (Herndon, VA: Alban Institute, 1998).

Chapter 2: Managing Personnel

1. Clearly, there are some situations that call for an extended (more than 6–12 months) interim period. Congregations undergoing significant internal turmoil or whose future existence is in question are definite candidates for extended interim pastorates. However, even with the former, if a new pastor comes into a

tumultuous situation and resolves it, won't she have a very successful ministry? In 1983, I came to Western, a congregation the Presbytery had already voted once to close. I don't think they needed to evaluate who they were and where they were going. They needed immediate, strong pastoral leadership.

Chapter 3: Managing Facilities

1. International Facility Management Association, definition, http://www.ifma.org/what_is_fm/index.cfm

Conclusion: Congregational Management

1. "Corner Office," *The Sunday New York Times*, November 1, 2009, Business, 2.

2. Henry Mintzberg, *Managing* (San Francisco: Berrett-Koehler Publishers, 2009), 13.